We Can Break
The Cycle of Child Abuse:
An Adult Study

Virginia Reese Kent

A Resource of the Section on Ministry of the Laity
General Board of Discipleship
In Cooperation with the Department of Human Welfare
General Board of Church and Society
The United Methodist Church

DISCIPLESHIP RESOURCES   NASHVILLE

Library of Congress Catalog Card No.:85-72114

ISBN 0-88177-021-3

WE CAN BREAK THE CYCLE OF CHILD ABUSE: AN ADULT STUDY. Copyright © 1985 by Discipleship Resources. All rights reserved. Printed in the United States of America. No part of this book may be reproduced in any manner whatsoever without written permission except in the case of brief quotations embodied in critical articles or reviews. For information address Discipleship Resources Editorial Offices, P. O. Box 840, Nashville, TN 37202.

Contents

We Can Break the Cycle vii

Introduction viii

PART I—THE PROBLEM xi
    1. The Scope of Child Abuse 1
    2. The Nature of Child Abuse 10

PART II—CONTRIBUTING FACTORS 21
    3. Child Abuser: Victim of Child Abuse 23
    4. The Isolated Parent 31
    5. The Special Child 40
    6. Chronic Illness of the Mother 50
    7. Other Chronic Problems 58

PART III—OUR RESPONSE 69
    8. Resources for Intervention 71
    9. The Congregation as a Change Agent 82

Glossary 91

Resources 93

Notes 96

With thanks to Art, my husband,
for his encouragement and assistance
in writing this study book.

We Can Break the Cycle

Child abuse and child neglect *are* preventable. Current legislation and judicial rulings are helping. Public and private programs of intervention and care are helping. But all these will be futile unless committed, concerned persons become involved in building a climate of love and care for all children.

A survey to determine the incidence of child abuse (including sexual abuse) and child neglect among United Methodists was conducted in the late 1970s. The results were shocking: United Methodists were involved as victims and abusers in almost the same percentage as the general society.

We cannot remain silent or inactive in the face of such pain in our communities and congregations. As United Methodists and as community citizens, we have a special responsibility to support positive adult/child relationships and to eliminate the conditions that lead to abuse and neglect. We have affirmed this crucial responsibility through our General Conference resolutions. We *can* prevent child abuse and neglect. With your help we *will!*

We commend this book for your study, discussion, and active response. Both the General Board of Discipleship and the General Board of Church and Society stand ready to help as you *choose* and *act* for better relationships among children and their parents in your community.

> BEVERLY ROBERSON JACKSON
> Director, Department of Human Welfare
> General Board of Church and Society
> The United Methodist Church
>
> EVELYN BURRY
> Director, Development of Lay Leadership
> Section on Ministry of the Laity
> General Board of Discipleship
> The United Methodist Church

Introduction

Child abuse and neglect have become common topics in the media. Newspapers and television news broadcasts have brought tragic stories to our attention, sometimes forcing us to look at an ugly side of human behavior that we would prefer to avoid.

For years, as a parent, I avoided the topic. I was appalled that anyone would actually seriously injure a child they had brought into the world. I wondered if I might have "abused" my children when from time to time I had found myself very angry with one of them and had spanked out of anger. For these reasons, I did not want to know more on the topic.

When I became a social worker, I found myself in the position of working to prevent child abuse and neglect. I discovered that the families with whom I worked were not so different from myself, except that their coping skills were limited and their support systems often non-existent. In addition, because many of the families I saw were poor or short of cash, they struggled with the problem of food, housing, and medical care at a subsistence level. In many cases, their problems were so longstanding that they lacked any concept that there are other ways of living.

Professionals working with such families have great difficulty in effecting a change in their lifestyles. It was discovered that non-professionals working with these families had greater success, probably because they were more available and invested themselves in the family situations from day to day. When these non-professionals were provided support by the professionals on a case, they could work together effectively over a period of time to help the family.

Occasionally, I spoke to church groups about the problem of abuse and neglect. I found these church people genuinely interested in helping. Gradually I began to think of the congregation as a natural resource of people who care about others. Why not, then, train these caring people, so that they would know more about the factors involved in child abuse and neglect and what they could do to prevent it?

These same church members live in neighborhoods where child abuse occurs. Since family violence is not exclusively a problem of a given neighborhood or race or economic group, no doubt it also occurs in church families. What an opportunity to be in mission for God! We can serve where we are, with eyes open to children and families who are hurting, by demonstrating that we care.

This book is written with several purposes in mind: to inform you about child abuse, to help you understand the factors that contribute to abusive parenting, and to stimulate you to think of specific actions you might take to help hurting families. If you are a parent, you may also be encouraged to find ways to improve your own parenting skills.

Because of the nature of child abuse, it is not possible to give actual case histories in this book. In no way would I want to reveal a specific family's problems so as to risk further hurt. Therefore, I have presented fictional but typical situations, so that you can get an idea of the many problems these families face. Through these fictional situations you can come to a new understanding of the potentially abusive family.

Note that there is a glossary of terms on p. 91. If in doubt about any of the medical or social work terms used, check the Glossary for meanings.

A Word to the Group Discussion Leader

The study of this book in a small group where the theories and situations can be discussed will be of greater value than individual reading. Members of the group will benefit most from reading a chapter before coming to the session where the chapter will be discussed. You can best prepare for the discussion by carefully checking the questions presented within and at the end of each chapter. Reword the questions as needed for your group members. If the number of questions seems overwhelming, choose to explore those that are more likely to help your particular group. Take the time to help group members get to know one another.

Role playing is suggested at various points. This technique is very effective in helping situations to come alive for purposes of a discussion. Those who agree to take a part can be given information about the background of the "person" they are to portray, but how they act the part is up to them. They cannot know the mind of another person, and that is not necessary. Encourage them to say whatever comes to mind. What happens in the role play situation is what the group then discusses. Try to focus on how it felt to be this person. In this way frustrations, anger, sadness, etc., will all come to light.

Before starting in the study, ask participants to share some good memories of the loving care they received as children. Ask those who are parents to tell a little about their children and perhaps share incidents of warm, loving family relationships. If you think it is wise, you may also call for sharing times of stress experienced by participants as children or parents, but it might be less threatening to save this until group members are more deeply related.

The use of a newsprint flip tablet can facilitate discussion by providing a handy place to record group responses. The very fact that something has been written seems to give it more weight. When the time comes to make decisions about a possible project, having that record of your sessions will guide discussion and action.

Do not be afraid to discuss thoroughly both the theory and the situations presented in each chapter. Try to understand where each person in a given situation is coming from. When there is disagreement among your group members, do not be dismayed. In fact, encourage those who disagree to share their feelings, always asking them to explain what they mean. Do not assume that you understand their meaning just because the words are familiar. When they cannot explain clearly, ask them to share an experience that will help the group understand. Often that type of sharing opens up a new understanding for people.

In fact, a good way to discourage confrontation when there is disagreement, is to request that people talk about their personal experience. Use of the pronoun "I" enables each to share his or her feelings without saying, "You're wrong and I'm right." We all have had different experiences and each was valid in its time and place. Bring the group back to the present, however: "Taking into account that this is a different person and different circumstances, how would you suggest that it be handled now?"

Finally, I encourage you, as leader, to assist your group in deciding what they want to do about child abuse and neglect. Choose a goal and lay out a timeline for completing it. Get busy while enthusiasm is high and momentum flowing. With your group, you can be an instrument of God to create a better world, a world of more love and less violence.

PART I
The Problem

Chapters One and Two introduce the basic information you need in order to understand child abuse. Chapter One provides the historical perspective. Child abuse is not just a present-day phenomenon; all forms of child abuse and neglect have been present since the beginning of recorded history.

Chapter Two describes the various forms of child abuse: physical, verbal/emotional, neglect and sexual. Each category of abuse has its own special way of hurting the child. Any of them can set up a reaction of loss of self-esteem and a warped view of personal relationships which persists into the following generation.

Chapter One
The Scope of Child Abuse

Child abuse has become a national problem of great proportions. In recent years the attention of the news media has made us aware of the apparent increase in instances of child abuse and neglect. Dramatic stories shock us: a baby fried in a pan, a retarded youngster kept locked away without access to sanitary facilities and fed the barest amount of food, and the outright murder of children! Daily papers and television bring these and other stories of abuse and neglect vividly before us. We wonder about the sanity of parents who could be so cruel to their own flesh and blood.

As a nation, however, we are ambivalent in our concern about child abuse and neglect. On the one hand, we report and are shocked by child abuse; on the other hand, one of our largest states, which budgeted $10,000,000 in 1982-83 for the prevention of child abuse and neglect, budgeted no money at all for this purpose in 1983-84.[1] Fortunately, the state legislature later funded a few programs. The child sexual abuse program in this state remains in the budget with no increase from the previous year's $250,000.[2] Early in the 1984 session of the state legislature, twenty-nine bills were presented.[3] Some of them passed, but the statistics continue to rise. If we are truly committed to prevention of child abuse and neglect, we will be putting more money into programs of prevention. Block grant monies from the federal government may also be used to fill the gap.

In addition to giving less financial clout to the issue, on the national scene certain congressional groups continue to push what is called the Family Protection Act. This act, in essence, would eliminate all shelters for battered women and abused children. It "seeks to prohibit federal efforts to stop child abuse,"[4] to preserve the family structure at the expense of the well-being of the individuals in the family.

Perhaps our national ambivalence is merely a reflection of our own ambivalence. We continue to be shocked by extreme examples of abuse committed by nameless people of our society. We would be disturbed if our neighbors were abusive, but we probably would not report the abuse. To get involved would be uncomfortable. Besides, we would not want outsiders poking around in our "closets," so we "respect" the privacy of our neighbors.

There may even be times when we become upset and strike our own children in anger. We may yell at them until they and we feel ashamed. We may fear that if we were to learn more about child abuse and neglect, we might discover that we are guilty at times. It is safer to distance ourselves from the problem. We believe that, as a society, we must punish those parents who seriously injure their child, but we do not want anyone telling us how or how not to raise our children.

Whether our own church members are experiencing violence in their families or not, we do share the same world as those who are violent, and it hurts us all. For children who are being beaten, the "real message is that when [they] grow big enough and strong enough, they too will be able to vent their anger by violent and humiliating attacks on other people."[5] Somewhere along the line, we are all affected by what is being done to others. The problem does not just belong to the poor or the criminals, or the uneducated; the problem affects all races, all religions, all socioeconomic levels of our society. It exists in our own neighborhood as well as across town.

If we believe that the church is a caring community of people who want a better world for everyone, then we are involved. We must not distance ourselves any longer. We must work through our own reluctance to look at the issue. We must become informed about what child abuse and neglect is and what it is not. We need to discover the causes and find out how to prevent it. This problem will not go away until we are all clear that it must be stopped.

Historical Perspective

In the early 1870s in New York, a social worker was visiting a client in a tenement when she observed a child named Mary Ellen who was obviously undernourished and had been brutally beaten. She was informed that Mary Ellen's guardians beat her regularly. The worker reported the facts to her superiors and to the authorities, who agreed that they did not have any legal right to intervene. Finally, the victim was drawn to the attention of the courts by the Society for the Prevention of Cruelty to Animals, which classified her as an animal for this purpose.[6] It was only after this that the Society for the Prevention of Cruelty to Children was established in New York,[7] and a few years later another chapter was established in Philadelphia. This was the first documented case of recognized child abuse in the United States. This was by no means, however, the first instance of child abuse.

From earliest times, in our Hebrew, Greek, and Roman backgrounds, certain abuses of children (including sexual) were culturally accepted and commonly practiced. In the Middle Ages, children were regarded as miniature adults, dressed as adults, and expected to work at an early age. The Industrial Revolution only worsened the situation by bringing in children to work under harsh and unsafe working conditions. In Victorian times the prostitution of early adolescents was rampant.

In the early years of the United States, we more often than not emulated the values of Europe. Our children were expected to work long and hard under unsafe conditions. Corporal punishment was common both on the job and in the home. No one questioned the right of the employer or the parent to beat the child. There was a reason no one was willing to accept responsibility in Mary Ellen's case, for it was commonly accepted that her guardians had the right to beat her, if they felt it was necessary to correct her.

There was a belief that physical punishment was necessary to maintain discipline, transmit educational ideas, even to please the gods and expel evil spirits. Parents, teachers, and employers were expected to use physical punishment when needed.[8]

Slowly but surely, reformers began to take up the advocacy of young children. Early social workers fought and won the battle against children working long hours. Eventually laws were enacted which protected children from exploitation by greedy factory owners. Schools were established, and children were required to attend. Schools, however, used corporal punishment when a child did not conform, and the image of a proper family was one where the father was the avowed patriarch, meting out discipline in the form of spanking with a paddle or beating with a belt. Our language even reflects this with the use of the term *belting* someone, whether a belt is actually used or not.

Recent History

In 1961, C. Henry Kempe, a pediatrician, first proposed the term "battered child syndrome" at a symposium. He had catalogued 662 cases in a single year, 27 percent of which were fatalities. Every state and every social class was represented in this group.[9]

With these figures in mind, Kempe proposed that every child suspected of having been abused be put through a battery of tests to determine the extent and confirm the diagnosis of child abuse. His recommendations are followed today in most large hospitals.

"A minimum of 3,000 children are killed by their parents every year in the United States. Over 750,000 cases of child abuse and neglect are reported annually."[10] These data suggest how reporting has increased our knowledge of what is going on. "At least one child in ten is a victim of incest."[11] These are shocking statistics. Perhaps our wonderment is that it has taken so long for these practices to prick our conscience enough to goad us into action.

Cultural Factors Today

Early Sexual Development

Children of previous centuries had little opportunity to be children, no opportunity to be adolescents, and from their early teen years, often assumed the responsibilities of parenthood. With the advent of public schools, that has changed. In our current society, children are usually encouraged to play as a means of preparation for adulthood. Adolescents may work to earn money, but in general, they are not encouraged to assume full responsibility for a child or even for themselves. Child psychologists believe that there is a natural progression of growth experiences which enable the child to become a responsible adult; when crucial stages are abbreviated or skipped, the chances for mature adulthood are slim.

Currently, however, there appears to be an increase in younger girls giving birth to babies. A recent report from a home for unwed mothers indicated that they had children of ten and eleven who were expecting babies. Earlier in this century puberty occurred at twelve to fourteen years of age. Now it is common for puberty to occur as early as ten years of age. Our national obsession with sex has even greater implications when girls this young are physically, if not emotionally, able to have babies.

The implications are frightening: children bearing children! It is hard enough to do an adequate job of parenting when the parents are mature adults. Our society is not set up to encourage children to assume the responsibilities that parenthood forces on them, nor should we. Young people who miss out on the important maturation of adolescence make poor parents.

Our Daily World

The world in which we are living causes us to experience greater pressures, perhaps, than at any time in the past. We live in a time of transition. Such a troublesome time causes us to re-examine our values and leaves us at a loss as to who we are and what we want. We have left the Industrial Age and moved into the Information Age. Most of us have little concept of what that means. The book, *Future Shock*, by Alvin Toffler,[12] presents a picture of what that does to us. It sets our society adrift, loosened from our roots and not yet established in new fertile soil.

The Eighties have provided a climate in which many of us are unemployed or underemployed, which demoralizes us and lowers our self-esteem. Today's climate differs from that of the Great Depression, in that our expectations are greater than they were then. The media have done their part to bring the world into our living rooms. Television commercials have taught us to expect more. Our homes reflect greater affluence. We are not satisfied with one bathroom—we want two or more, plus a fireplace and wall-to-wall carpeting. In short, we are not satisfied with the simple life any more.

Sex has become a commodity promoted in movies and television, in our slick publications and in commercials. On the one hand, we want our children to wait for sex until they are mature enough to deal with the emotions and the responsibilities. On the other hand, they are daily bombarded with provocative women and men selling products on television. The movie industry seldom produces a film which does not reflect this obsession with sex and sexuality. Our children are in a double-bind created by the so-called adults of our culture. They are told not to have sex but are faced with visible enticements to the pleasures it promises.

Modern Women

Women are becoming parents at both an earlier and a later age. Younger and younger girls are experimenting with sex and ending up with babies. Yet many women in their twenties are trying out new roles for themselves—taking time to pursue their own careers, discovering what experiences provide satisfaction to them aside from home and family. Some of these women have now reached their thirties. Recognizing that they are approaching a biological boundary line, many of them are having their first child after the age of thirty, and some after the age of thirty-five.

Just as there is no ideal time for every woman to become a mother, there is no guarantee that every woman will enjoy parenting. Ariel Swartley, one of those women who made a conscious choice to have a child after thirty, very much liked the idea of becoming a mother. She went into the situation with her eyes wide open, determined to approach motherhood in an informed manner.

She was surprised to discover that there is no way to prepare emotionally for the experience. She says,

> The terrifying moments are the ones when your teeth clench and the thought of one more spoonful of carrots flipped casually on the rug by a testing one-year-old is enough to make you scream; and it is, and you do, and suddenly screaming isn't nearly enough and your head swims with the desire to punish this offender who has dared interfere with your life. The line between control and losing it is so thin, and it often seems that the only way to keep the rage within safe limits is to load yourself down with guilt for even feeling it at all.[13]

Most, if not all, mothers have had those feelings. I suspect that the pace of modern life, the expectations laid on women and men, and the pressures we all feel combine to make a relaxed parenting experience difficult, if not impossible. We all need help!

Baby and Child Care

Dr. Daniel Gottlieb Moritz Schreber, 1842-1911,[14] was an early adviser on child rearing. He regarded babies as "untamed badness." They were the "adult's natural enemies to be suppressed and moulded."[15] This man promoted a program to teach children to obey, which might be likened to brainwashing. One of his sons went mad, and the other committed suicide. In spite of this, his were the only views on child rearing available to parents during much of his lifetime and many years beyond. He believed that disease resulted from badness and health from good behavior.[16] It was he who first insisted that children clean their plates. Discomfort was considered to be good for children.

In 1946 Benjamin Spock published his first edition of *The Common Sense Book of Baby and Child Care*.[17] It proved to be a liberating force. For the first time, parents were urged to treat their children like human beings. Since that publication, Spock has been accused of promoting permissiveness, which he denies. The fact remains, however, that many parents did become permissive after reading his book. This has provided us a different type of problem—the child/adolescent who recognizes no authority at home, at school, or in the community.

Books on child rearing have proliferated since that time. We have been deluged with books on how to talk to our children and teenagers, how to enhance their self-esteem, how to discipline, how to listen. Some of these authors have even held seminars to teach instructors who in turn offer the course to train parents in one technique or another. For the first time, perhaps, we are free to learn from a variety of methods that can assist us in being effective parents. Hopefully, we will not wait to learn these skills until we are so alienated from our children that even these skills will not bring us together.

Conclusion

Most all parents may at some time or another be tempted to abuse their children. In general, however, there are certain factors that contribute to the likelihood that parents will be abusive. When we identify these factors and locate families who exhibit these problems, we label them "at-risk," meaning that they are especially vulnerable to family violence.

"Primary preventive efforts must take great care to insure that the label 'at-risk' does not precipitate or in any way contribute to the problem it predicts."[18] This means that although we acknowledge, by labeling them, that these families have a greater tendency toward violence, we must take care not to send the message that violence is expected. Labeling is always a two-edged sword. While it enables the helping community to be supportive, there is a stigma attached which implies an expectation.

Child abuse and neglect *can be contained*, but it will not be an easy task. While we must address the problem of abused children in our society, we must at the same time address the issue of prevention of abuse in future generations. "Prevention as a general concept means to identify and reinforce people's strengths and to identify and remove pathogenic factors in people's physical and social environments."[19] Mental health professionals cannot do this on their own. They need the concern and action of everyone.

The Role of the Congregation

The congregation has an unprecedented opportunity to make an impact on child abuse and on prevention. As the traditional preserver of the family, the church needs also to be concerned about the individuals in the family and the quality of life fostered there. Along with educators and child psychologists, church people should unite and encourage at least these three preventive measures: (1) the preservation of a safe and sane childhood for our children, where children know that they are loved and valued as worthy persons; (2) education to prepare children and youth to make intelligent choices regarding parenthood for themselves; and (3) preparation for parenthood when the time is right.

Self-understanding is an essential ingredient for adults. We have access to materials that help us to understand and accept our own strengths and our limitations. There are trained professionals who lead groups and teach courses that assist us in achieving this understanding. Our churches can make use of these resources to help us attain this goal.

Knowledge about child development is available and within reach of everyone through schooling, libraries, and our congregations. When we understand ourselves, know about child development, and make use of birth control, we have the basic knowledge required to make an informed decision about becoming parents.

If we are parents already, we can always learn more about ourselves and our children. We can increase our communication skills to the point where we enhance the relationship we already have with our children.

We certainly *can* do these things! Will we?

Over and above these things, we can learn more about child abuse and neglect and assist professionals with preventive techniques. As you read this study book, you will probably learn things about yourself and your relationship with children, your own (if you are a parent) or others. Most certainly you will learn about the problems of child abuse and neglect and how you can become a part of the solution to this serious problem.

For Thought and Action

1. Now that you have read about child abuse and neglect in a historical perspective, share with your discussion group any other stories

you have heard about cultural practices which are really abusive to children.

2. Agree as a group that each person will be responsible for bringing in reports on child abuse or neglect from the newspaper, radio, or television.

3. Your study will be enhanced if several people agree to read and report back on *The Best Kept Secret*, by Florence Rush, and *The Sins of the Fathers*, by Ruth Inglis.

4. Brainstorm ideas about concrete services your church might provide to help prevent child abuse. Keep the list and compare it with your brainstorms following Chapter Seven.

Chapter Two
The Nature of Child Abuse

The trauma of the abuse that children often endure is daily laid before us in the newspapers and on television. It is easy to get caught up in sympathy for the helpless infant or the dependent child who seemingly is a victim of her or his parent's anger or frustration. It is also easy to feel outrage against adults who burn, beat, neglect and/or sexually abuse their dependent offspring. While it is easy to understand that parents do get angry with children, it is difficult to understand how they can lose control and actually injure their own children.

Public reaction to abuse often results in the separation of parent and child. Certainly this prevents abuse from recurring. But it is painful for the child as well as the parent when this happens. The ultimate goal needs to be primary prevention, so that separation need never occur in the first place.

To reduce child abuse significantly, it is necessary to be able to identify potential abusers. When it becomes possible to locate these individuals and work with them before they become parents, child abuse may really be reduced.

The purpose of this study book is to begin to get a feel of how and why some parents abuse their children, and discover some ways to prevent it—rather than to focus only on the child. Why is it one parent abuses and another parent does not? What makes the abuser different from the non-abuser? In some ways they are alike; and in other ways, they are a world apart.

Before we examine the factors which make child abuse likely, it will be helpful to understand more clearly just what constitutes child abuse and what forms it takes. This chapter will provide an overview of the four general areas of child abuse: physical abuse, emotional/verbal abuse, sexual abuse, and neglect.

Physical Abuse

Physical abuse is the type we are most likely to see reported in the news. It is dramatic and often shocking. This type of abuse, which may leave physical evidence of the parent's behavior, is what often starts a wave of indignation resulting in new laws and new social work positions to deal with the problem. Other forms of abuse and neglect may be every bit as traumatic to the child, although not as obvious to an observer. Each kind of child abuse may leave lifelong effects on the personality and, conceivably, an inability to deal with normal adult life.

Bruises

Bruises are common among children. Most children in the course of normal play will fall, hit their legs on some object or be hit by other children, and bruises may result. Toddlers fall frequently and may have bruises on their face or bumps on the head. Children who are bruised by adults, however, have in addition to typical childhood black-and-blue marks, multiple bruises on their torso, all in various stages of healing. A fresh bruise is red, later turning blue-black and still later turning yellow-green.

These bruises are often in the form of a handprint where the adult has struck the flesh of the child. Wraparound bruises are caused by the use of cords, belts, or ropes which are flexible enough to curve around the body and leave a distinguishing mark. Rulers and other types of sticks leave a distinctive mark, as do teeth when the child has been bitten. Occasionally these instruments will lay open the skin and cause deeper injury.

Children of school age who are subject to this type of abuse may be observed wearing long pants and long-sleeved sweaters even on warm days. Neither the child nor the parents want the bruises to be observed.

Caution needs to be taken in diagnosing child abuse by bruising. There are some medical or genetic conditions which will cause the same effect. Babies born of Asian and Spanish extraction are occasionally born with "Mongolian spots." These spots are blue in color and usually found on the buttocks. They fade when the child is five or six years old. Until that time, they can easily be mistaken for bruises.

There are also blood conditions in which what appear to be bruises may practically cover the body. Even physicians can make the mistake of diagnosing incorrectly. Children have been removed from their home on the basis of multiple bruises only to discover belatedly that they suffer from a blood disorder. These families suffered unnecessary distress because the current emphasis on child abuse causes some pediatricians to react before they check carefully.

Burns

A second form of physical abuse commonly seen is burns. Any toddler is subject to the likelihood of being burned by a furnace or kitchen stove. Deliberate burns are another matter. An abusive parent may punish a child who is being toilet trained and has an "accident" by dunking his or her buttocks in scalding water. A misbehaving child may have a hand or foot held under the hot water tap or in a pot of hot water until a deep solid burn occurs to "teach them a lesson." Sometimes a lighted cigarette tip or flame is used as a form of punishment.

Broken Bones

Other forms of physical abuse are not so obvious to the untrained eye. The use of X-rays and diagnosis by technicians and pediatricians can spot hairline fractures of the long bones (arms and legs) indicating instances when the bones were broken and healed without medical attention.

"Most injuries are incurred not so much by direct blows as by vigorous handling, as in shaking the child. . . . Infants under one are the most frequent recipients."[1] Trauma to the joints may unavoidably occur when the parent grabs an arm or a leg to keep the baby from falling. Such trauma to the joint may also occur when the adult pulls or twists the arm or leg to make a point to the small child who is irritating him or her.

Due to the pioneering work of C. Henry Kempe, pediatrician, trauma centers now run a battery of tests on any child suspected of having been abused. Those tests include a full set of X-rays and careful diagnosis. Only when several indications are present will child abuse be a likely diagnosis.

There is some speculation that mental retardation may occur occasionally as a result of a neck injury caused by shaking an infant. Not until a number of months after birth can an infant hold up its head. Until that time, parents must take care to support the head when lifting the baby. The neck continues to be fragile for some time. When, unfortunately, a baby is fretful and cries long and hard, a frustrated parent may be inclined to shake the baby with considerable force. As a result, the baby may suffer whiplash, just as the automobile accident victim who is thrown violently forward and snapped back. The infant, however, is more vulnerable to brain damage. Parents need to be cautioned that there may be a cause-and-effect relationship between shaking an infant and subsequent retardation.

Verbal/Emotional Abuse

In most states, there is no legal way to remove children from a home merely because they are subject to verbal assaults, name calling, yelling, or "double-bind." The "meta-message" (unspoken but implied) from parents is that the children are bad, lazy, careless, and/or stupid. The bottom line is that the children come to believe themselves to be unloved and unlovable.

A "double-bind" occurs when a parent says one thing to the child, but behaves as though the opposite were true. For instance, a child is punished for fighting another child, but the parent who punished is heard bragging to another adult about how strong and tough the child was in the fight. Such a double-bind also occurs when the parent is inconsistent in expectations. On one occasion the child is allowed to behave in a certain manner, and on another occasion the parent flies into a rage when that behavior occurs. Such inconsistency is confusing to the child. If the double-bind message occurs often enough, eventually children will come to believe that there is something wrong with them, because they cannot be sure of pleasing their parents.

In families where two parents consistently give different messages, children survive by becoming manipulative and playing one parent against the other, or they may go to the opposite extreme, becoming confused and withdrawn. In both cases, the children believe there must be something wrong with themselves.

Under situations of marital stress, it is not unusual for one or both adults to take out their frustrations on the children. The anger they feel toward one another can be misdirected toward the child. The psychological term for this is *projection*. Projection is more likely to occur when the child bears some resemblance in looks or behavior to the parent who is the true object of the anger. The child invariably thinks that she or he is to blame. Children think of their parents as wise and capable adults, whether that is true or not. If a "wise, capable adult" is sending messages that the child is lazy, stupid, nervous, useless, or bad, the child reasons the adult must be right.

Imagine this information being recorded on a cassette tape in the child's mind. If the message is recorded over and over, it becomes established as "truth." Later, it will replay at crucial times and that individual will act as though he or she were lazy, stupid, nervous, useless, or bad, whether it is true or not. Self-esteem, so crucial to successful adaptation in adult life, may easily be short-circuited by a parent's cruel words repeated often enough.

Sexual Abuse

Sexual abuse includes the full range of sexual touching, from stroking the breasts and/or genitals to actual intercourse. Boys as well as girls may be the victims. Small children who are frequently allowed to observe sexual intercourse of adults are in jeopardy of failing to learn that sex, rightly used, is an expression of love between two adults who respect and care for one another. Some small children exposed to sexual scenes come away with the impression that the only way they can earn the affection of adults is to copy what they have seen. Provocative behavior on the part of young children may be indicative of their premature exposure to sexual activity.

What is your reaction to what you just read? Are you shocked to hear that children frequently exposed to scenes of sexual intercourse may be confused as to behavior expected from them? The frequency with which a child is exposed, the attitude of those whom he or she observes, and the framework of love and affection, or disrespect and anger, all contribute to whether such exposure may be considered abuse or not.

Children have a natural curiosity about sex which should not be confused with deliberate exposure to overt sexual activity by adults in their lives. Children playing doctor together are in a different category from the child who is taken by a parent to observe sex between teenagers or adults. Children who have been removed from their homes by authorities due to such behavior on the part of their parents often have a hard time working through their feeling that to be accepted they must behave sexually.

There is disagreement over the proportion of girls who are sexually abused compared to the number of boys; whether the trauma is equal; whether child molesters are to be considered normal or psychotic; and whether the child victim encourages the sexual behavior of the adult or not.

There is little dispute, however, that 80-90 percent of the offenders are male, that 80 percent of the offenders are family members or close friends, and that only a small percentage of the actual incidents are reported. There is abundant evidence indicating that incest and other sexual abuse take place on all social, economic, and racial levels.

Florence Rush, in her book *The Best Kept Secret,* reports that "more than one-half of all victims of reported rape are under 18, and 25% of this number are under 12. 70% of all prostitutes and 80% of all female drug users were sexually assaulted in childhood by relatives."[2] Recent reports also indicate that an extremely high number of men and women currently in prison admit to having been sexually abused as children. We cannot be sure whether they would now be in prison if they had been brought up in a home free from sexual abuse, but there is no doubt that this was a contributing factor in bringing them to their present condition.

"I have never knowingly talked to a happy, well adjusted, unconcerned incest victim,"[3] says Dr. Suzanne M. Sgrai, former chairperson of the Sexual Trauma Treatment pilot program in Hartford, Connecticut. The statement was made in response to the suggestion that early sexual experience may not be harmful, a notion that persists in spite of evidence to the contrary.

As women who were sexually abused as children begin to feel freer to talk about their experiences, we are beginning to learn what it is like to live in a home in which fear is a constant companion. While girls are more frequently sexually abused by a father or stepfather, other male relatives are occasionally to blame. Older brothers, uncles, grandfathers, and respected family friends may also be culprits. Dependent upon family for food and shelter, these girls sense that something is not right about what they are expected to do, but they often will not jeopardize the family by revealing the facts.

It has been documented that children as young as eighteen months have been sexually abused, long before they have any understanding of what is happening. One girl I learned of had a hysterectomy at six years of age after several years of sexual abuse by a family member. Another woman finally carried a baby to full term after multiple miscarriages which her obstetrician was convinced were caused by the sexual abuse she endured as a child.

Discussion

What are the elements of fear that you suspect keep many young girls and boys from telling on family members who sexually abuse them? What do you think children can do when the persons they tell refuse to believe them? Frequently fathers who abuse their daughters are widely respected men of their community. What means might a man use to insure himself that his daughter would not reveal his indiscretion?

Medical Consequences

There are "indisputable concrete physical hazards"[4] of early intercourse. The obvious consequences are venereal diseases and early pregnancy. Teenage pregnancy is risky. Complications are more likely to occur during pregnancy and birth than with the woman in her twenties. Maternal mortality is 60 percent higher for women under fifteen years of age.[5]

Less obvious problems are rectal fissure, lesions, poor sphincter control, lacerated vaginas, perforated anal and vaginal walls. Death by asphyxiation and chronic choking from gonorrheal tonsilitis is almost always due to sexual abuse by adults.[6]

Emotional Consequences

It is not at all uncommon for children who have had sexual experiences with adults to believe that there is a connection between the sex act and their own worth. These are the children who may be said to be seductive.

"Denial or mitigation of the problem leaves the victim alone to bear . . . the burden of this shameful secret and its consequences."[7] Other likely reactions to being sexually molested are depression, inability to perform the usual tasks of each day, resistance to attending school, loss of appetite, bedwetting and nightmares, and lack of friends their own age. At the end of the spectrum are those who develop psychoses and those who commit suicide.

At best, adult sex with a child is a betrayal of trust. The child is robbed of the protection and love that the adult might have provided. The parent who abuses is not a protector, and the other parent, who for whatever reason does not prevent it from occurring, is also failing to protect. Unfortunately, it sets the child up to spend his or her entire life looking for and never finding that elusive parental figure.

The women's movement can be credited with helping to bring to public awareness the enormity of this problem. At last women are encouraged to talk about what has been forever hidden.

The use of children for sexual purposes in myth and history has been common. A mistaken impression has been perpetuated by the attitude that such behavior on the part of men was excusable. Even some psychiatric circles have tended to blame the wife for ignoring man's need for sex, forcing him to seek out his daughter; or they have blamed the child for being seductive. For some unexplained reason, the adult man is often not held accountable by our society as a whole for his own behavior. This seems to imply that men lose all sense of judgment when it comes to sexual matters. It seems to hold women and children responsible for men's actions, which is a curious twist when you think about it.

The reasons a man " . . . seeks out a child as a sexual partner is because a child . . . has less experience, less physical strength, and is more trusting of and dependent upon adults and therefore can be more easily coerced, seduced, lured or forced."[8] The child also would likely not know whom to tell outside the family. On the few occasions that children have revealed incest, they have often not been believed.

A small percentage of these cases involves adult women as sexual abusers. Less information is available about these cases.

Neglect

There is little written material about neglect as an aspect of child abuse. Perhaps that is because we are so reluctant to intervene in the lives of other families who appear to be functioning adequately except for the behavior or appearance of their children. Perhaps it is because neglect does not have the obvious physical scarring effect on the child that other types of abuse engender. Even when complaints are checked out by authorities, nothing much occurs unless there is a clear and present danger to the children.

Neglect may take many forms: medical, emotional, nutritional, or environmental. Medical neglect occurs when the parents do not take normal precautions against disease, or when they do not follow the instructions of their physician regarding follow-up care. Children with rheumatoid diseases, diabetes, etc., need frequent monitoring to remain as well as possible. Physicians are required to report cases where the health of the child is endangered by the parent's failure to comply with the medical regimen. This is a difficult decision for a physician to make.

By using the courts to force the parents to comply, a delicate balance in a multiproblem family could become totally upset.

Nutritional neglect occurs when, for whatever reasons, the child does not receive a balanced diet. The parent may not have nutritional information and/or may not be able to afford proper food. A child who is overfed is in the same category.

Failure to Thrive

On occasion, when a home provides an atmosphere in which one or more of the children fail to develop within a normal range of physical growth, social awareness and ability to walk, talk, etc., they may be suffering from "failure to thrive" (FTT).

Failure to thrive is a syndrome found in infants and small children. When the normal increases in height and weight and head circumference do not occur, the child is checked for any number of causes. If none is found, the baby may be placed in a hospital where regular meals, emotional support and attention are available. The parents are urged to be there as often as possible. Their interaction with the baby is noted and suggestions made to improve the connection between parent and child. If the child begins to gain weight and grow normally, FTT is diagnosed. The cause is then considered to have a connection with poor quality of physical and/or emotional care given in the home. In short, this is neglect.

When these FTT children are identified, an interdisciplinary team from the medical and social work communities can assist the family to begin to function in a more regulated and consistent environment. Many of these children tend to be extra-sensitive to the emotional climate in the family. Once family members are aware of the problem, with help they can provide the stability the child needs to grow.

Summary

Whatever form abuse takes—physical, verbal/emotional, or sexual abuse, or neglect—it is harmful to the child. Children are dependent upon their parents to provide the safety and love which make possible continuing growth. Those for whom this environment is missing are likely, years later, to become parents who do not know how to provide a healthy environment for their children.

The numbers of runaway teenagers are increasing. These are the young people who often become drug addicts, or they become prostitutes or thieves to support themselves. For that reason, shelters for teenagers have been given some priority funding. In these shelters we are learning that a high percentage of youth have run away because they were abused by their parents.

What about these parents? What kind of "ogres" are they? Probably 99 percent of them want to be good parents. Only a very few are psychotic and cannot be helped. Most of the others function on a scale of very well to very poorly.

In the next few chapters, we will study why it is that some parents find it difficult or impossible to succeed at parenting. We will examine the specific factors that have been identified as often present in cases of child abuse. Sample situations will be introduced to illustrate typical problems. Ask yourself what might have made a difference for the individuals in the situation—such as the interest of a neighbor, involvement in a youth group, etc. Above all, try to consider what we as a society, and more particularly as a church people, can do to make a difference. Is there not something you can do for even one person caught in situations such as these?

Each situation presents a unique combination of factors. Abuse might not occur if one of the circumstances is changed.

For Thought and Action

In small groups of two or three persons, share answers to these questions:

1. Have you ever taken a child to a doctor with a bruise that was difficult to explain? What was the reaction of the physician? Did she or he believe your explanation?

2. In raising or caring for children, what kinds of situations have caused you to feel overwhelmed? How have you resolved the problems?

3. What were your childhood experiences? What method of discipline was used on you? Were your parents always fair or logical, or were they sometimes irrational?

4. Have you ever reported an incident of child abuse or misbehavior of a child to the police? What happened, and how did it work out?

5. If you are a parent, how did you obtain the necessary information for raising your children? How did you learn about nutrition? Did caring

for a baby come naturally, or did you have to learn from someone else? Who taught you? How did you learn?

6. What resources are available in your neighborhood for young mothers to learn about caring for their babies?

7. What are the laws in your state regarding corporal punishment? (In some states it is legal for parents to spank their child, but they may not bruise the child. In some states step-parents do *not* have the right to spank their step-child.)

8. What methods do you know for correcting children without using physical punishment? Find out about Logical Consequences (Dreikurs)[9] and the No-Lose Method (Thomas Gordon).[10]

9. What organizations do you know that provide classes on parenting? Is there a local chapter of Parents Anonymous, a self-help group for abusive parents? Is there a local self-help group for incestuous families? What are the philosophies of these groups? Ask representatives of these groups to come speak to your study group.

PART II
Contributing Factors

The following five chapters are designed to examine the various factors present in different cases of child abuse. No certain factor guarantees that a family will become abusive; however, there are a number of problems that run like a familiar strain through many cases. Never does one factor alone precipitate child abuse; rather a combination of some of these five factors is always present:

1. *Abusers were abused:* Eighty percent of all child abusers were abused when they were children. As a result they (1) lack successful parental models and (2) missed out on nurture needed for healthy self-esteem.

2. *Isolation:* Child abusers are isolated. They may lack social and communication skills, and fear people. They tend to have dependent personalities and may look to their children to provide the love they need. As a result they and their children experience *role reversal,* in which the parent acts as the child, and the child takes on the parenting role. Or they experience *symbiosis,* in which the bond between parent and child becomes too close for healthy functioning.

3. *The special child:* Frequently the abused child looks or acts differently than the rest of the family, or looks or acts like a family member who is disliked. Premature babies and chronic medical problems suffered by children both create special stress situations which may result in abuse of the child or siblings.

4. *Chronic illness of a parent:* A parent—especially a mother—who is chronically ill can prevent the family from functioning normally. Mental illness and drug abuse are also included in this chapter.

5. *Other chronic problems:* Crisis is often the "norm" for the abusive family. Many of these families live through crisis after crisis with only brief calm between the "storms." A related factor common in many cases is the parent with a personality problem. The inability of an adult to contain anger and hostility, to assume responsibility for a dependent child, to maintain steady employment, and to function within the law is often the result of a personality problem. These character disorders not only affect the adult, but seriously impinge on normal family functioning. Even worse, they instill in the child antisocial patterns which will likely persist into the following generations.

As you read Chapters Three through Seven, notice how many of the above factors are present in the typical situations examined. None of the situations presented will fit neatly into any one category. This is typical of families who are at risk for abuse.

Chapter Three
Child Abuser: Victim of Child Abuse

The parent who is abusive can be better understood when we begin to look at the life story back of that parent's upbringing. Although a short temper, low tolerance level, and multiple problems can make a person more susceptible to becoming abusive, what is often seen in these parents is a childhood in which they were abused physically and/or emotionally.

Children who are abused often grow up to become abusive parents. Such children are not absolutely certain to become abusive parents, for too many other factors may influence that outcome. On the other hand, empirical evidence (relying on experiment or observation) clearly indicates that 80 percent of parents who are abusers were abused as children.[1] While one study indicates that only 30 percent of abusive parents rate their own parents as having been abusive, unquestionably their childhood was "characterized by adverse or traumatic experiences to a significantly higher degree than non-abusers."[2]

If, in addition to the above, the family of birth lacked sufficient food, clothing, shelter, education, and/or nurture, the child would be called "multi-problem," suffering deprivation and with unmet basic needs. Upon becoming adults, children subjected to abuse and deprivation may well "suffer from poor ego development, . . . low self-esteem, low achievement level, identity confusion, and high frustration."[3] "Despite all these scars, there is often a burning desire on the part of these parents to want things to be different for their children, . . . they just do not know how to make it happen."[4]

There are several life experiences which make it possible for children to grow up and assume the role of healthy, loving parents: adequate role models, sufficient nurture from parents who convey the idea that they are worthwhile individuals, and parents who care enough about them to see that they get the basic necessities of life, including plenty of love. But when parents are inadequate in any way, they may perpetuate their inadequacy when their children become parents.

Role Models

Whether child abuse occurs hand in hand with deprivation or not, the child of an abusive family does lack a primary source of role modeling for parenthood. Of course, the primary source of role models is our homes. If our parents are inconsistent, abusive, unloving, cruel, or neglectful, for whatever reason, we miss out on an extremely important opportunity to learn successful parenting skills. A secondary source of role models may be television, which, more often than not, presents skewed models of people who are funny, dangerous, sarcastic, or so perfect that the viewer cannot relate to them.

A third possible source of role models for parenting is the family next door, or the family of a friend, or even a teacher at school. Why one child uses only his or her family as a role model, while another child is able to find suitable role models outside the family of birth, is hard to explain.

Just as some children seem to be born full of energy and enthusiasm while some are born passive, content to sit and play quietly, so some look elsewhere to learn about the world and others are content with what their family offers. Some parents are more protective and allow their children little opportunity to venture forth from their homes, while others encourage or at least allow their children a full range of experiences.

The combination of the adventuresome child and the protective parents, the passive child and the encouraging parent, or any one of a number of additional combinations in between may set the stage for accepting or rejecting the parental model.

Abusive parents who were abused as children are probably ones who either passively accepted the abusive model from their parents, or, while rejecting the form of their own abuse, now choose another means of punishment for their children, a means that they do not recognize as abuse. For example, beaten as a child with a thorny switch, now as parents they may lock their child in a dark closet for hours at a time.

Raised with harsh discipline, physically punished whenever behavior is unacceptable to their parents, and with little love to compensate, children grow up without a model of nurture and caring. Such children who become parents may treat their own children as they were treated. The form of discipline they received as children may be rejected, but they have received clear messages that children are supposed to conform to the parents' expectations upon demand. When their children behave as children often do, by overt misbehavior or subconsciously react with bowel or bladder problems, the parents may interpret this as willful disobedience. True to values learned as children, such parents may severely punish the children for failing to live up to their demand. If their parents used a stick to hit them, they may use a belt. If their parents used a belt, they may use their hand to vent their anger and lose control of the severity with which they strike.

When such parents have no partner who can intervene, it is possible for child abuse to occur. These parents may see themselves as different from their parents, because they truly love their children and often express this love. But they lack the objectivity to discern that the punishment they use may be as harmful as that of their own parents.

For Discussion

Discuss the following in your group. How permanent are the values with which a child is raised? When unloved and/or harshly punished children later become parents, do they inevitably behave in similar ways? Can you think of exceptions?

As you think about the childhood of abusive parents, what influences could have made a difference in the values they retained? Of course, you will find no conclusive answers, but you probably will come up with several possibilities.

Outside of your family, who has had the greatest influence in helping you set your values? Share with your group a story or two about such people.

Ask yourselves if there are children with whom you now have contact to whom you might be providing adult role modeling. Are there children in church who might be aware of your actions? Do you have neighbors with children who notice how you handle situations? Are there other children with whom you have contact and who are learning from you?

Nurture

A basic ingredient for growth is the knowledge that you are loved. When parents fail to express affection, and give their children few signs that they are accepted and loved, these children will be emotionally deprived. Let us use the words *nurture* and *lack of nurture*. "The ultimate benefits to the child accrue when his or her parents receive the caring they need: only then are they in a position to respond to their child's needs."[5] People must be nurtured as children before they can nurture their own offspring.

Adults who were abused as children often were never given an opportunity to be children. "To become independent, one has to have been permitted to be dependent."[6] When a child is expected to perform adult tasks—such as comforting parents, preparing meals, tending smaller brothers and sisters—to the exclusion of normal childhood activities, that child has not been allowed to be dependent and, therefore, will have difficulty becoming independent.

An important aspect of maturity is the willingness both to be responsible for oneself and to relate with other responsible adults. In addition, parents must be willing to be responsible for their dependent offspring. Overly dependent adults are unable to be responsible for themselves, much less for their children. Nurture is unknown when the parents are dependent types.

To nurture is to promote growth. Children grow in more ways than physically. They need to grow emotionally and socially. They need to increase their knowledge, wisdom, confidence, and competence. Can you think of other ways children need to grow? Nurture of children, then, includes providing opportunity for all these facets to develop; encouragement to try and try again until they succeed; and underlying all, the confidence that they are loved by their parents. When opportunity, encouragement, or love is missing, the child lacks nurture. The child may grow up physically, but when such children become parents, how can they provide nurture when they have never experienced it?

Role Play

If you are using this study in a group, the best way to get a feeling of what it would be like to live in a family where the mother was not nurtured as a child would be to role play a situation. If you are reading this on your own, read over the role play situation. Use your imagination to put yourself in the action. Take a few moments to become each character and see how it feels. Ask yourself what you would do if you were that person in that situation.

If you are in a group setting, plan to role play this situation together. Choose someone to play the part of the mother and another person to play the part of the child. Those who play the roles are encouraged to be spontaneous and not worry about what someone else would do or say. In enacting such a role, let the words come. Whatever happens will give the group plenty to think about and discuss.

The Mother: The mother in our first typical situation was reared in a family where the parents were constantly fighting. Since she was the oldest, she was expected to act the role of parent to the younger siblings. This meant that she was not able to participate in peer activities at school or after school.

Now she is a single parent of a preschooler. She drinks to forget her loneliness. She has no contact with her own family. She has no friends and is afraid to initiate contact with her neighbors. She lives in self-imposed isolation.

Two-year-old daughter: The two-year-old daughter has been kept inside and not allowed to play with other children ever since she was old enough to be interested in others her age. She is a normal, active child who wants the attention of her mother if she cannot play outside.

The situation: In this situation, the little child from the next apartment is outside and the daughter wants to go out and play, or she wants mother to read the seventh story of the day. Give the mother and the child names and allow them to enact a scene.

Discussion: How did it feel to be a mother of a two-year-old who demands attention all the time? How did it feel to be the daughter of a mother who will now allow you to play with other children?

Add a volunteer to the scenario: Try another scene with mother and daughter. Only this time introduce a volunteer. Give her a name and tell her that she will have a year to become the friend of this mother, teach her about the needs of small children, and help her find friends with whom she can feel comfortable.

Enact a scene where the volunteer is getting acquainted and being friendly to the mother. Let the child be a normal, active child.

Discussion: How did the volunteer feel trying to be friendly to a person who is very reticent? How did the mother feel with a stranger being introduced as someone wanting to be a friend? How did the child react to all this? How did the volunteer react to the child?

Think about this mother. What part did the lack of nurture in her formative years play in her expectations of herself as a parent? At what point in her early years might an outside person have been able to make a difference? Child abuse and neglect often go hand in hand. In what ways was this mother both abused and neglected in her early years? As an adult, do you suppose she is depressed and/or has low self-esteem? The "unpredictable moods of depressed parents may lead them to praise the child on one occasion and seem oblivious on another."[7] This presents a double-bind which is very confusing to the child. Such parents have "an attitude of hopelessness and helplessness because of not knowing how to cope, or even what to cope with, and consequently raise counter-barriers of hate, fear and often self-hatred."[8] As parents we often repeat what we observed our parents do when we were children. It may result in our unhappiness and depression, but until we are able to recognize and accept help, it is very difficult to change.

Continue to use your imagination. Think for a moment how Christ would view this mother and child. What do you believe is the Christian approach to dealing with this situation?

Neglected Children Become Neglectful Parents

Studies seem to point to neglect as a generation-to-generation pattern.[9] There is every reason to believe this, especially when we isolate the factor of neglect from that of abuse. The abused child suffers from overtly cruel behavior on the part of the parent. The neglected child rarely is aware of what is missing. This child has the same choice of parenting models as any other child, but more than likely has come to accept as normal the pattern of benign neglect demonstrated by the parents. "Child neglect may be due more to deficiencies in mothers' nurturing knowledge and behaviors than in their purposeful withholding of care."[10] Information and demonstrations help, but the need is that of changing the way of dealing with life, a difficult transition when properly motivated—nearly impossible, if not.

Neglect seems to be more prevalent than outright abuse, but it has had less study and less understanding than other forms of abuse. Neglect occurs within intact families, but it also occurs among children who are in custody for one reason or another. However much effort is put into making their lives as "normal" as possible, there is nothing "normal" about living in an institution or in being shifted from one foster home to another. These, too, may be counted among the neglected. Foster children often become parents who neglect.

Emotional Neglect

Children are often placed in foster homes due to traumatic situations. They may be removed from their homes for a variety of reasons, but when a tragedy occurs in which the family is broken by the death or desertion of parents, the child may never return to a "normal" home situation. Sometimes siblings are not placed in the same foster home, and as a result the family is further split. If for some reason the child is never accepted for adoption, that child may be periodically shifted from one foster family to another. Survival becomes an important skill to learn and can become an obsession.

When these children who survive foster placement grow up and marry, they may lack an understanding of the need for emotional nurturing on the part of their children. After all, they survived without it. The values they esteem are survival and security, and if they can provide those for their children, they feel good about that. When there is a marriage partner who can provide nurturing, perhaps no harm is done. When, however, there is no partner, or when neither partner is equipped for nurture, the children may suffer emotional deprivation, a form of neglect.

This situation would not likely ever come to anyone's attention unless the family were to experience some unusual period of distress, such as the loss of a job by one or both parents and the accompanying need for rent and food money. At such a time, children may act out the distress of the parents with overt behavior problems, frequent tears or nightmares. Remember, the parents are survivors, but the children are not. In addition, the children lack the nurture they need to provide a sense of emotional security in their lives.

Points to Ponder

What do you know about the foster parent program in your community? What special training is given to foster parents to assist them in dealing with children who have survived trauma such as the death or murder of their parents or desertion by their parents? What are the criteria for determining whether siblings will be placed in the same foster home or be separated?

If these child victims of family trauma and breakup grow up to have their own families, they may expect their children to "be tough" and survive and may not recognize the necessity of emotional nurture. As parents, how can they be enabled to respond to their child's desperate need for affection and emotional security?

Children who suffer from emotional neglect are without role models. They have not been allowed a normal childhood, not been able to depend upon a reliable, loving person in their life. As parents, they may find it extremely difficult to be the nurturing parent their children now need. How can our society provide remedies that will help these parents become more nurturing? How can your congregation? How can you?

Summary

All children need to be secure in the feeling that they are loved and lovable. They deserve to be treated with respect, even when they misbehave and must be corrected. How they are treated will be, more than likely, the way they will treat their own children. Parents with serious deficiencies in their background find it difficult or impossible to parent successfully.

This is not to say that persons who have suffered these deficiencies cannot adapt in adulthood. They often develop very strong coping skills and even have been successful in significant ways. Unfortunately, our society promotes parenthood for all, so most of these formerly abused and neglected people choose to do the accepted thing and become parents. It is here that problems may arise. When they lack a proper role model, lack the nurture all of us need to be able to be nurturing, and lack basic knowledge about children, these parents are missing vital elements in a successful parenting process. When, in addition, they face a crisis, their failure as parents is likely to become obvious. Armed with an inheritance of abuse and neglect, they each try to do their best as parents. We, in our society, failed them in some way, and we continue to fail some of the abused children of today who may be tomorrow's abusive parents.

For Thought and Action

1. Share responsibility for finding out what resources are available in your county to (a) care for abused children; (b) assist parents in developing parenting skills; and (c) help foster parents to deal with children who have suffered trauma.

2. Discuss what you might do if you suspect a neighbor of abuse or neglect of a child. (Refer to Chapter Eight.)

3. If you have a child abuse hotline in your county, find out what happens when a suspected case of child abuse is reported. If possible, have a social worker come from the agency to speak to your group.

Chapter Four
The Isolated Parent

Isolation is a "disease" afflicting our American society. Nowhere is it more harmful than in the parents of small children. In some ways, these parents are more vulnerable to its grip. All parents are familiar with the demands children make upon their time and energy, leaving little time to relate with other adults. Babies need almost constant attention to feeding, bathing, loving, and changing diapers. Toddlers must be guarded against tempting but dangerous areas in and around our homes; we must see that they have proper clothing and adequate, balanced meals.

In addition to the demands of small children, there are normal household chores that are important for safety as well as aesthetic reasons. Other members of the family also demand equal time and attention from the wife/mother, husband/father. These demands can keep parents from connecting with other people in the neighborhood.

Ours is a very mobile society, with one out of every four or five families moving each year. Moving places the family in greater jeopardy of isolation. More than likely, the moving family knows no one in the new neighborhood. There is often no extended family (grandparents, aunts, uncles, cousins) nearby.

Isolation is one of the prime factors influencing parents to use abusive measures with their children. "The nuclear family household . . . lacks the support of alternate caretakers; mothers who are unable to break continuous contact with their children are most likely to behave more punitively toward them."[1]

If the family does not join a church or other caring institution, if there is no available car in working order, and if parents do not know how to negotiate the bus system, the household may be immediately isolated. In fact, even having a car and joining a church do not guarantee against isolation.

Isolation can take many forms, but in the potentially abusive family, isolation may be divided into three types: emotional, economic, and social. Most persons have experienced one or more forms of isolation sometime during their life. What makes one family different from another is the manner in which members react to isolation. Some have learned to reach out, while others fold into themselves, increasing their loneliness.

Emotional Isolation

Emotional isolation occurs when we are unable or unwilling to share our feelings with others. Married couples may experience this when one partner or the other is extremely busy, or when one lacks the skill to express feelings. It may also occur when one partner lacks self-esteem, believing that her or his feelings are unimportant.

The opportunity to air our feelings often aids in the development of coping skills. Being free to speak out about something that is bothering us invites feedback. Even though we may speak out in anger, the feedback can help us think about the problem in a new way. When that feedback is missing, because we are bottled up emotionally, or there is no other caring adult available, it is difficult to develop new coping skills.

Role Play

Using the role play techniques outlined in Chapter Three, act out the following situation. If you are reading this on your own, imagine yourself as each character in turn. Whichever way you do it, try to get a sense of the feelings involved.

The mother: In this role play pretend the mother is still a teenager. She was raised by her aunt who used excessively harsh discipline. As a young girl whenever she tried to make friends, it seemed as though she was not wanted. Consequently, she has many hurtful memories and no friends.

At a very young age she married and moved across the country to get away from her home. A baby was born the first year of that marriage and is now a year-and-a-half. The husband has many friends, but she still is afraid to try to make friends with other women. She knows little about the development of babies and children. She hesitates to attend classes because she might get hurt again when she tries to make friends.

Right now she is frustrated. Her one-and-a-half year old will not settle down to nap, and is crying. The father is watching television and drinking beer.

The father: This man had a good enough upbringing. He has several friends. He was attracted to his wife because she seemed so helpless and needy. He wanted to be the strong, kind person she was seeking.

This father has a steady job which pays fairly well. He expects his wife to take care of their apartment and their child. He is beginning to feel tired of being responsible for keeping her happy. She always expects him to talk with her when he is home. He does not want to be bothered.

The child: The one-and-a-half year old daughter in this family senses that something is not right between her parents. She also knows that if she cries enough, she will get her mother's attention, even if she is spanked. She is active and wants to be busy.

The situation: It is Saturday afternoon. Mother has put in a full morning doing household chores and is ready to sit and talk with father. This is the first time in a week that they have had time to relax together. Mother wants to tell father how hard it is for her during the week and that she wants him to help with their daughter. The child is crying because she does not want to nap.

Choose three persons to play the parts. Give them names. It does not matter if a woman plays the part of father, or a man the part of mother.

Discussion: Let each of the persons who played the parts share what it felt like to be the person portrayed. What were your frustrations? How did the rest of you feel toward this mother, father, and child? How do you think you could help this mother if she were your neighbor? Chances are she never has learned how to relate successfully to people. As a neighbor, it might be very difficult to remain friendly to her.

If you were a volunteer who was aware of the difficulty this mother has in relating successfully with others, how would you approach her and maintain a relationship?

Do you know men who do not understand their wives' needs to talk to other adults? Do you know men who refuse to participate in caring for small children? What can be done to help these men to understand how important both of these needs are for women, as well as for the children and the men themselves?

When a mother is unable to express her feelings directly to anyone, male or female, the only person to whom she can safely direct her anger is the child. The child might react as this one did by refusing to nap and crying. What other ways might a child react? Are any of these reactions ones which might cause the mother to respond with abuse?

Some small children try to become the "adult" caregiver their parent needs. If they succeed and are called upon often enough in this capacity, they are robbed of their chance to be children. If they fail, they may be vulnerable to abuse.

A trained volunteer could attempt to provide some nurturing of such a mother and at the same time provide a safe avenue for ventilation. The volunteer needs to also remain sensitive to the child's need to be free of verbal and physical abuse. Volunteers can model good parenting skills and encourage parents to learn more about child development. Do you have the patience to become such a volunteer?

Economic Isolation

Economic isolation may come as the result of trying to provide for a family while lacking sufficient resources to maintain a lifestyle to which the parents are accustomed. Possibly both parents work long hours at the cost of developing friendships outside the family. When crises occur, coping skills are minimal and the family may not know where to turn.

Economic isolation comes, also, to many on Aid to Families with Dependent Children (AFDC) whose income is barely enough for survival, or families with one wage earner near minimum wage when they do not have budgeting skills, or when extra expenses have become overwhelming. These families are frequently very mobile. Some are periodically evicted for failure to pay the rent; others move hoping to improve their surroundings. Each move necessitates having enough money to pay the first and last months' rent, plus deposits for cleaning and security. They seem to lack the reasoning ability to see that they are getting further and further behind. On the other hand, these families have few possessions, so moving is more easily undertaken.

In areas of the country with a relatively mild climate, some families have been known to use a campsite for a base. They stay the maximum two-week period before moving to another overnight park. The children may or may not maintain some kind of regular school attendance. Other families live in their cars, whether or not the vehicles are operable.

In every part of the nation a growing number of families are located in motels. The family crowds into one room, adding kitchenette privileges if their budget can afford that. Motels do not require first and last months' rent, and the security deposit is small. The motel provides enough furniture, including a television set to entertain. In some motels, the use of a phone may even be included.

Most motels allowing families to stay on a semi-permanent basis are run down; still they provide minimal shelter. Unfortunately, many of them are also host to persons who use and/or push drugs and prostitutes. A family in such a setting can stay and become a part of the scene, stay and keep to themselves, or move. Under the best of circumstances, however, it is difficult to keep children quiet in one small room. If a parent was abused as a child, is now isolated, experiencing a crisis, and confined to a close environment, the abuse of children is almost inevitable.

Role Play

The following role play presents one of many types of situations faced by families who use hotels or motels as a home. While each family who lives in a motel or hotel is different and the circumstances that reduced them to this economic level differ, the isolation that occurs is real and further exacerbates their tendency toward abuse.

The mother: Imagine a mother of twenty-five years. She has been married twice and has four children. The first child was born when she was sixteen. This mother is thin and cannot seem to gain weight. She is obviously nervous. She is resentful of the many responsibilities she has and wants to make up for her lost years of adolescent freedom.

The father: Father is the same age as his wife. Although he has valuable work skills, he is unable to hold down a position for more than a few months at a time. He has a low boiling point, and occasionally loses his temper and becomes violent.

The children: The children range in age from two to eight years. You can decide which are boys and which are girls. One of the children may be in need of glasses, but there is no extra money to afford the eye examination and the cost of eyeglasses. Mother has not been willing to see if the county would provide those services.

The middle two children are very active; the oldest and youngest are more passive. They are living in a motel, and the two middle children prefer to play outside with other children living there. They are noisy and disruptive.

The situation: Father stopped on his way home from work to get drunk again. He is frustrated with their lives. They once had their own apartment, but he lost his job. They had no financial reserves, so when he found another job and could not afford the first and last months' rent plus deposit, they were forced to move to one room and kitchenette in a motel.

He feels responsible for his family, but he seems unable to provide the things they need. He knows that mother is forced to put up with a difficult situation, but in his frustration, he blames her for not being more supportive of his situation.

Choose people to play each of the parts and give them names. Let each participant read the description of their character and get into the feeling of being that person. Set the scene in the motel room, and let them enact whatever comes up for them.

Discussion: Where do your sympathies lie? Can you understand the mother's feeling that life is passing her by? Do you understand the father's frustrations? Talk about what you think it might be like to live in one small room and struggle with a situation you feel powerless to change. What types of solutions can you come up with now?

The characters in this role play have a number of factors contributing to the likelihood of verbal and physical abuse and even neglect. The father drinks too much and is often violent when he drinks. The mother is struggling with identity issues which are usually dealt with during adolescence. One of the children is having a problem with eyesight. The family is isolated. They have no support system, no caring extended family, no friends. Without caring persons in their lives, they have no opportunity to ventilate except in an escalation of violence within their family, and no incentive to develop coping skills.

In some cities social services agencies provide a special service to families living in motels. Is this a problem in your area? Does your local social services agency acknowledge and provide special services to these families? Does your ministerial association know about these families and provide a ministry? It is something to think about. What can your congregation do?

Social Isolation

Emotional and economic isolation often results in social isolation. There are forms of isolation, however, that have to do primarily with the person's inability to interact with anyone on a social level. Some people have never learned how to make social contacts. They experience stage fright, and consequently they deliberately avoid contact with their neighbors. If they attend church, they are not likely to initiate friendly conversation. They avoid small group meetings where they might be called upon to say something.

Other people suffer from occasional or frequent bouts of agoraphobia, "the abnormal fear of being in open or public places."[2] These people are actually afraid to leave their homes. When a mother of small children has agoraphobia, she will not even shop for food. Shut in a confined area with children for several days, she may become a victim of her own frustration, and take it out on her children. Such parents are likely to develop a neurotic symbiotic relationship with their children. B.F. Steele describes faulty symbiosis as a "conviction, largely unconscious, that children exist in order to satisfy parental needs. Infants who do not satisfy these needs should be punished . . . to make them behave properly. . . . It is as though the infant were looked to as a need-satisfying parental object to fill the residual, unsatisfied, infantile needs of the parent."[3]

Symbiosis starts as a natural interdependency between a mother and her newborn infant. The mother awakens at the first whimper of the infant and rushes to determine what the baby needs, and then provide the dry diaper, milk, or whatever. In a sense, symbiosis at this time is "meeting mutually shared needs: the infant's need to be nurtured and the mother's need to nurture."[4]

In maturing, the child moves from a dependency to independence. If the position of dependency is maintained past the level when the child needs the parent to perform certain tasks, the child never learns to meet his or her own needs in a satisfactory manner. Then the dependence becomes exploitive and neurotic.

"Malfunctioning symbiosis can be attributed to instances where parenting is inadequate to prepare the child to function as an independent person who can solve problems in the world."[5] Later, when this child becomes a parent and is still seeking someone to fulfill his or her needs, role reversal may occur, in which the parent expects the child to satisfy needs of the parent. When the child is expected to comfort the parent on a regular basis, the child can never be a child and the parent is not an adult.

For Discussion

To make this type of situation more real, let us imagine a single-parent family. The mother was raised in several foster homes and has no extended family to count on for support, nor has she had steady role models to teach her parenting skills.

The mother: The mother is agoraphobic, which means that she is fearful of being among people. She often stays in the apartment for days on end, requiring the daughter to do what must be done outside of the home.

The child: There is one child, an eleven-year-old daughter. She has transferred to a different school every year for the past three. They are seeking a better apartment.

Daughter shops for mother and is expected to wash windows and mop the kitchen floor. She is also expected to listen to mother's problems. In her resentment of these expectations, mother and daughter often bicker.

Sometimes the daughter disappears several hours at a time. When she returns, the worried mother and her daughter usually have verbally abusive fights.

Discussion: List the problems you see in this family. How does symbiosis play a part in the interaction between mother and daughter? Is mother realistic in her expectations of the eleven-year-old?

Make a list of the changes that need to be made to assist this family in changing their verbally abusive pattern. Now make a list of possible methods of making these changes. Could a trained volunteer make a difference? How would that volunteer go about helping this family?

Summary

The separation of isolation into three types—emotional, economic, and social—is artificial, but the distinction is made to help you see that isolation has several forms. The important thing to remember is that whatever form isolation takes, the results are the same. The family is separated from any meaningful contact with persons who could give feedback and stimulate growth and change. Additionally, in emotional isolation, an individual may be separated from others in the family because of his or her inability to express feelings.

Isolation is a situation that can be remedied, relieving an important stress factor in the lives of some families. This is an area in which church people can be instrumental in breaking the cycle.

For Thought and Action

1. With another person, review one of the role plays in this chapter and share your feelings about the characters. Write down a few key words that summarize your feelings and share them with the rest of your group.

2. Tell another person about a time when you felt isolated. What were the circumstances? How long did it last and how did you get past this phase?

3. If a person was helpful to you during this period, who was it—friend, relative, stranger? Have you taken time since then to help someone in similar circumstances? Whom do you know now that you might help bring out of isolation?

4. What type of help can you give to a person who is isolated? Talk about ways you can approach a person who seems to prefer to be left alone. Maybe you will need to overlook certain rude responses they give when you approach them. Maybe you will need to go to them and just be a friend rather than inviting them to some group that you enjoy.

5. Could your church provide training sessions in how to listen and reach out to people? What else might your congregation do out of concern for isolated persons?

Chapter Five
The Special Child

There is a tendency to place all the blame for child abuse on the parent. The parent is the adult, and society expects the adult to be in charge. Of course, there is no guarantee that adulthood means an ability to control temper or to suffer frustration more easily than a child. It is to be hoped, however, that anyone who has become a parent will have learned some skills in working and communicating with others. In addition, the parent needs patience, love, and basic information on child development.

The child, however, often plays an unconscious part in his or her own abuse. Something in the personality, looks, temperament, or peculiar problems the child brings may block parents' ability to cope with a particular child. That child may become a victim of abuse or neglect, depending on the circumstances.

The Premature Infant

Who in their right mind would abuse a premature infant? Yet having a premature baby is extremely stressful! The parent may not be in his or her "right mind." In fact, the stresses associated with a premature baby and birth defects are so great that an unstable or insecure family is not likely to survive intact.

Children's hospitals are frequently tertiary care hospitals for premature infants, which means that in a given metropolitan area any premature infant with complications receives specialized treatment there. Parents often must travel miles to visit their infant. Upon arrival, then, the wee baby is confined in special equipment that ensures regular breathing, and may be connected with tubes to provide nourishment and blood. There are times when picking the infant up is impossible and any touching, which is encouraged, has to be done through special portholes.

These parents live with fear that the infant will not survive. Often the way they cope with that fear is just not to visit. To visit would be to deepen the bond with the child, making death more difficult to face.

Much is said these days about bonding. In general, bonding is described as an emotional connection between parent and child, which is stronger the sooner it occurs after birth. Hence, newborns are often placed first on the abdomen of the mother rather than being immediately taken to the nursery. More and more fathers are being encouraged to be present at the birth.

"Infants or toddlers are described as being at-risk if developmental lag is observed or if developmental, social or emotional problems can be anticipated because of the failure of the mothering person and the child to enter into a relationship that is growth producing for the child."[1] Parents of premature infants are denied these moments of emotional connection. The life of the baby is at stake, so thoughts of bonding are secondary to providing the medical necessities to sustain that life. Sadly, there are times when bonding does not occur at all. The child may then be vulnerable to becoming the focus of the parents' frustrations.

It is generally accepted that premature infants have a developmental lag in proportion to the amount of prematurity at birth. It begins to be understandable that a parent—particularly one who was abused as a child, or is isolated as an adult, or who has not learned to curb a temper—will find the stress of caring for a premature infant to be frustrating. This may lead to shaking or otherwise harming the child.

Typical Situation

Consider for a moment one typical family with a premature baby. The mother is single. Her parents will have nothing to do with her. Her sister talks with her but is in no position to help financially.

This mother's first child was a normal birth. When the first child was just over one year, mother had a second child. This one was premature and had a digestive tract that was not connected. Surgery was performed and the connection was successfully made. After taking the baby home with her, the mother had to make an emergency trip back to the hospital when she stopped breathing. This is a precipitant to Sudden Infant Death (SID).

Mother was given a monitor which buzzed when the baby failed to breathe. She had to rush to her at such a time and shake or otherwise stir the baby to start her breathing again. As you can imagine, this was a real stress producer for mother.

Mother is friendly and makes friends easily, but her friends seem to all be in circumstances similar to hers, without a car or a job. Her only income is from AFDC.

The baby is typical of premies and develops slowly, so mother is kept on a very demanding schedule much longer than most mothers are with young babies.

The older child is now four and the younger almost three. This second child, however, is still a little slower than the older one was at his age. In addition, the little one is mischievous. She does not listen well to mother and often does not obey. When mother becomes frustrated with her and tells her to behave, she does not pay attention. Only when mother uses a switch to spank her does she obey, and then she quickly forgets.

For discussion: What do you imagine it is like to have a premature infant requiring a major operation? Imagine some of the emotions you would feel if your child stopped breathing periodically and had to be shaken to start breathing again.

Have you ever had a child who would not listen and obey? How did you handle it? What do you think about using a switch on a three-year-old who does not listen when her mother speaks to her? If the switch does not leave a mark and manages to stop her long enough for you to make her listen, would you go along with this type of punishment? Why or why not?

This mother loves her children. How can she be helped? If she wants to get off welfare and earn a good living for her family, how can she be helped to do this? The government used to provide assistance to allow parents to be trained on the job and still receive the financial help to make it possible. That program is no longer available. Is there something the congregations in your community could do to help such young parents?

The Different Child

Sometimes there is one child in a family who stands out as different. Perhaps the child is blond or redheaded when the rest of the family is brunette. Sometimes the child is hyperactive. Sometimes the child reminds the parents of ugly Aunt Suzie, or disagreeable Uncle Charlie, or of some of the parents' own worst traits. Since children are born with personalities, a personality clash may even develop between parent and child. We may think that our own children should be born with personalities similar to ours, or with which we are compatible. There is no such guarantee.

As parents, we used to be told that we were responsible for our child's personality. Our children were likened to a lump of clay which we were to form, or a blank record on which we placed the life pattern. Thank goodness, we have passed that phase of child psychology! That is a terrible burden for any parent to face.

Now we believe that our children come to us with certain set personality traits. Our task as parents, then, is not to bend these characteristics to our control; rather, it is to learn what traits are there and use them to assist the child to live and work with others. We as parents have to do some changing to adjust to the new personality, and we can assist the child in making adjustments necessary for the enrichment of life. At least, that is what the successful parent will attempt. But what of the multi-problem families? How can they function successfully when, in addition to other stresses, they have a child who clashes?

"To say that a child's behavior is a primary precipitant of an abusive incident is not to say that the child is primarily responsible for the abuse. However, it does indicate that the child's behavior is a significant factor in the occurrence of abuse."[2] The parent's first response to misbehavior on the part of the child may be a warning. When the child does not heed the warning, gradually the parent becomes more and more frustrated, and may tend to use physical punishment. The types of behavior which are likely to bring on parental abuse are "aggressive behaviors (usually verbal), lying, stealing, defiance, crying, behavior involving food, elimination, and sleeping."[3] All parents are familiar with the frustrations that arise with these situations.

The Autistic Child

Let us look at one situation which may not be considered common, but does occur. A child is born who frequently becomes rigid and screams. On other occasions the child seems to be totally unaware of events occurring around him or her. These symptoms occur almost from infancy, but maybe the parents do not allow this to concern them until it becomes clear that the child is slow in developing speech.

When there are other children in the family to compare with, the parents may begin to worry that this child is retarded. Perhaps their pediatrician reassures them that this child may be a little slow, but not to worry.

The child may seem to be exceedingly hostile toward the parents at times, and their patience may be tested. Sometimes the child may babble and wave the hands in a rhythmic pattern which baffles the parents.

If they are lucky at this point and find a pediatrician who understands autism, they may learn something about the problem and how to deal with it. Then the parents may very well blame themselves for passing on a genetic defect or be blamed by a professional who is convinced that autism is a result of parent-child interaction. In either case, the parents go through a difficult period of self-blame.

Autism is not always easy to diagnose. Let us say that a case had been diagnosed. It is now necessary to establish a medication to help maintain the child more or less in a balance between hypo- and hyperinteractive. A medication that works for a given child may become ineffective and have to be changed from time to time.

As soon as possible the child will benefit from a preschool specifically designed to assist such children in adapting to the rest of the world. Chances are this child will need special schooling the rest of the school years. Many school districts are required to provide classroom experience for autistic and other exceptional children. In other school districts such a specialized class may not be available.

How can parents weather all the stress and worry and self-blame that come with the discovery that their child is autistic? How do they keep from losing control with a small child who seems so hostile and difficult to manage? If this family has marital or financial problems in addition to the stress this child produces, the potential for abuse is there.

Autism can be confusing, challenging, and heartbreaking. It is often misdiagnosed. As one parent said, "When we were finally given the correct diagnosis, it was as if we were told the child we thought we had died and that we had a new child in his place—a new child whom we had to understand, whom we had to learn all over again to live with and to love."[4]

Not all small children who are severe behavior problems have autism, but a few of them do. What resources are there in your community to assist parents with such problems? Do you tend to blame the parent when you hear of a small child who acts beligerently? Talk about your feelings. What kind of support system could be put in place to assist a parent with this type of problem? What could your congregation do?

The Ill Child

There are many chronic illnesses which afflict children and add considerably to the stress in a household: asthma, diabetes, cancer, heart ailments, cystic fibrosis, etc. In several diseases, emotional stress exacerbates the symptoms of the illness. In other diseases, the symptoms seem to be independent of emotional stress, but the demands of trips to the hospital or the doctor, medication, physical therapy, occupational therapy, etc., place tremendous stress on family life and resources.

Diabetes Mellitus

Diabetes does not deform or otherwise physically mark its victim, and a diabetic can usually participate in most activities. In more than any other chronic illness, however, the diabetic experiences a direct connection between life's experiences and emotions and the ability to keep the disease under control. There are inevitable periods of stress, anxiety, and anger. The teenage diabetic may rebel by refusing to stay within the dietary requirements or "forgetting" to take insulin.

Diabetes is considered to be inherited, and brought on by emotional stress. A newly diagnosed diabetic may be overwhelmed, frightened, and doubtful that he or she can deal with insulin shots and a rigid diet.

Parents of young diabetics will experience the same feelings, plus a sense of guilt for having passed on the hereditary defect.

Diabetes is controlled by a restricted diet, insulin injections, and exercise. Regular meals and rest are also required. Patients must maintain their own control. There is the possibility of diabetic coma from lack of insulin, or an insulin reaction with too much. In short, this can be frightening to both parent and child.

In an otherwise well-adjusted family there will still be periods of frustration and resentment, but if the family has other stresses, the disease is often used by either parent or child to gain an advantage. This serves only to further exacerbate the situation.

It sometimes becomes necessary for the child to be placed in the hospital in order to provide an emotionally neutral place where insulin can be adjusted. The parents may visit but are not encouraged to stay with the child under these circumstances.

It is easy to understand the stress with which these families with a young diabetic have to deal. In addition, "over-protection and over-anxiety can accentuate the child's sense of handicap and may be an expression of hostility"[5] on the part of the parents.

In diabetes and other chronic childhood illnesses, "well-meaning efforts of staff and family to compensate young patients for the discomfort they are experiencing by giving them presents and special privileges may afford them so much secondary gain that they find more immediate gratification in remaining ill than in becoming emotionally committed to the long, often difficult, struggle to regain their health."[6] These children may become manipulative, using their pain (illness) to provide themselves favored status in the home and hospital. Parents who frequently feel guilty that their child is not healthy, may easily be swayed to provide special privileges for their ill child. Siblings, too, may be enlisted to perform tasks for the ill child, who might be better served by having to perform the task alone.

Role Play

A family with three children is on AFDC. The children range in age from five to thirteen. The middle child is diabetic and is currently in the hospital to stabilize her insulin.

The child is a favorite of the nurses, and she sometimes takes advantage of that. In general, however, she tends to become depressed when she realizes that the diabetes is not easily coming under control.

The mother has not visited for over a week now, and the child is saddened about that. She does not understand what is keeping her mother from coming. At home, she gets all her mother's attention. She even gets privileges that her siblings do not.

The mother: The mother of this child is single. She is trying to get off AFDC by taking a secretarial course. To visit her daughter, she must take a long bus ride of two hours each way. If she visits at night, she must leave the other two children alone, because she cannot afford a sitter.

This mother is still young and attractive. She makes friends easily. Once in a while she can get a ride with a friend, but usually the friend is not available.

There is no phone in the house, so she cannot receive messages from the hospital except through an acquaintance who is not reliable.

This mother feels a great load of guilt. Maybe it is her fault that this child is so ill, she thinks. She knows she ought to visit her more, but her job training and her other two children are important, too.

Situation: Choose someone to play the part of the mother and someone to play the part of a nurse who is talking to her when she finally telephones to inquire about her daughter. Let them sit back to back, for if they were on the phone, they would not see each other. Have the nurse try to explain how important it is for her to be there every day for the sake of her daughter. Have her explain that the disease can be made worse if the child is upset. Let the mother respond in the best way she can.

Discussion: How did the mother react in this situation? Was she defensive? Did her guilt increase? How would you have handled the situation? What would your priorities have been under the circumstances?

As an outside person, what do you think would have been most helpful to this mother? Is there something that you or your congregation might do to assist her in this situation?

In families where chronic illness claims the attention of parents, guilt always plays an important part, as does grief over the loss of the image of a physically perfect child. Guilt often produces one of two reactions: Either the parent devotes all attention to the ill child and neglects the others; or the parent resents the ill child and takes it out on some other member of the family.

Prolonged hospitalization has a profound effect on the family structure. If the parents visit frequently, other parts of their lives must suffer. If they are unable to visit very often, they feel even greater guilt. They may not visit at all, because to do so permits their guilt to surface.

Medical Neglect

It is not unusual for a parent with a child needing frequent checkups at a children's medical center to miss appointments. When a child seems to be healthy, and getting to the clinic means making special arrangements for transportation, it is easy to skip an occasional appointment. Some clinic hours necessitate traveling during heavy traffic hours, which makes it even more difficult. "When the medication prescribed alleviates the disease, families tend to minimize its intensity and thus delay seeking the best treatment."[7] The psychological term for this is *denial*. Denial may be the most common defense used by young patients and their families. In a typical denial, the parents probably feel that the child has improved, and that the trip to the medical center takes more planning and effort than it is worth.

Under some circumstances, pediatricians decide to report cases of medical neglect. The court, then, may choose to put the parents under a legal requirement to see that the child appears regularly at the clinic.

What is your reaction to the fact that some parents skip appointments? Do you believe the physician should always report the case to the authorities? Elaborate on your answer. What effect do you believe such a legal order might have on family relationships?

Summary

Even conscientious and well-functioning parents may be faced with a situation beyond their control, such as a premature child with birth defects, or a child with neurological problems or chronic illness. When these parents have a good support system, a loving relationship and no survival issues, such as lack of food or shelter, they may manage well through the additional stress. If, however, they are experiencing other problems in their lives, the additional strain may cause family violence, or more likely neglect.

As a result of guilt feelings about producing a child who is not physically perfect, and the stress of prolonged medical regimen or hospitalization, "all parents have some resentment about the extra care and responsibility required by the . . . child. . . . In some instances, the child himself may be resented and rejected."[8] Sad but true, and also very human. This statement was written about the diabetic child, but might well be used to describe any child with a chronic disease.

Sometimes nothing can be done to change the course of illness for these children already suffering from various childhood illnesses, but we can be aware of the family stress and provide services to alleviate that stress in some way.

Social workers are employed at children's hospitals to work with families in maintaining a balance of some sort. When the families come regularly to the clinic or to visit their hospitalized children, such psychosocial treatment can be very helpful. If they do not come, treatment is much less effective. Sometimes volunteers are available to provide transportation.

Some of the national associations that assist people with various diseases have support groups to enable families who are affected by the disease to share and emotionally support one another. Congregations often provide space for these groups to meet.

For Thought and Action

1. Talk about the various problems faced by parents of premies, chronically ill children, and other special children. What volunteer services might be helpful? What additional financial resources might be secured?

2. What are some of the stresses associated with cystic fibrosis, cerebral palsy, diabetes mellitus, Juvenile Rheumatoid Arthritis? What other chronic diseases do children suffer from, and what are some of the ways parents manage to keep from being overwhelmed? Have you had a chronically ill child? What are some of the resulting stressors? How important is a support system? When there is no extended family nearby, how can a support system be developed? Can you or a group of people from your congregation provide a support system for a family with an ill child? How will you go about it?

3. What is the reaction in your church groups when a child of one of the parents present is disruptive? Do you tend to blame the child or the parent? Does the parent end up leaving the meeting with the child? How can you and the groups you attend in church gatherings be more supportive to such parents?

4. Have you had or known a hyperactive child? What is it like to be the parent of such a child? Does your church offer Parents' Day Out, so parents can have some change of pace away from their child? Perhaps this would allow them some refreshing experiences so as to return to loving care of a difficult child.

5. Contact local offices of national disease associations and local children's hospitals to inquire about the need for transportation assistance to families with a chronically ill child. Do they need more volunteers? Take the responsibility for presenting this need to the entire congregation and enlist new volunteers for the hospital or disease association.

6. In what other ways can you or your congregation become involved with these families who have special children? What would it take to carry out one of the ideas? Do it!

Chapter Six
Chronic Illness of the Mother

In Chapter Five, we took a look at special children who, for reasons sometimes beyond their control, are a source of frustration for their parent(s). One type of special child is the child suffering from chronic illness. The parent is pressed to choose attention to that child over other priorities in life, such as other siblings, marital considerations, etc. In some instances, the parent and child never bond, and as a result the relationship tends to be more impatient and less affectionate. In other cases, the parent lavishes attention and affection on the child to the exclusion of other children in the household.

In this chapter we will investigate situations in which it is the parent—especially the mother—who suffers from a chronic disability. We will look at three disabling problems: physical illness, mental illness, and substance abuse. We will see how this can affect the children and make them vulnerable to abuse or neglect. Even intact families with stable incomes, may be affected dramatically by these factors.

Physical Illness

The impact on a family when the caregiver is ill varies with the type and severity of the illness, the drain on energy used in traveling for treatment, and the drain on the pocketbook. As with childhood ills, there may or may not be a direct emotional connection. The strain may come from fatigue, worry about the children as well as the mother or other caregiver. Some illnesses are difficult to diagnose—such as food allergies, which can cause sufferers to experience times when they feel as though they are "going crazy."

When there are children to be considered and no outside arrangements can be made for child care, the ill parent is forced to continue to cope with them while feeling physically or mentally unable to cope. If there is no extended family available to assist, or those that are nearby are too old or do not understand the stress the parent feels, the problem is exacerbated.

Role Play

Imagine an intact family with three children. Father often works overtime. The children in this family are two, four and six, and the middle one is especially mischievous.

The mother: Mother used to work, but her health and emotions have been so precarious that she has quit. She has some friends that she can phone and talk to when she gets depressed, but gradually those friendships are wearing thin.

Mother's physician is unable to tell her what is causing her symptoms, and tests are under way to determine the cause. When she is not feeling well she worries about her health and tends to be impatient with the children. She finds that she yells at them often and then cries in shame at her own behavior.

The father: The father is often tired after work. The last thing he wants to do is come home to an upset wife and children. He often tells mother to get her emotions under control. He urges her to do a better job of keeping the house clean to occupy her mind.

An evening conversation: This evening, mother is trying once again to explain to father that she needs help. She tells him about her day and the way the children misbehaved. She says she spanked the four-year-old and then cried for an hour. She is sure that her illness is serious, if only the doctors could discover what is wrong. Father tries to be sympathetic, but he wonders if she is just imagining her symptoms.

Choose two people, give them names, and let them talk. See if the mother is able to convince father that she needs help, or if father is able to convince her that nothing is wrong except that she is overemotional. Stop the conversation if one convinces the other. If no one appears to be convinced, stop the conversation after a few minutes. If you are reading this alone, try writing out a scenario, or try getting into the inner feelings of mother and then father.

Discussion: What is your evaluation of this situation? If you could control one of the characters, what would you make him or her do?

Let us imagine that time has passed. Mother has discovered that she has a debilitating illness which will be with her the rest of her life, without getting better but probably no worse.

Let the parents hold another conversation. Father is still tired from having to work long hours and somewhat resentful that mother cannot help out with a job. Mother is still adjusting to her illness and trying to accept that she will never really feel well. The marriage is beginning to be in distress. What happens this time?

What types of outside help do you think this family could use? Is there something your congregation provides—such as family counseling, Parent's Day Out, or people who are willing to make regular phone calls—to relieve the pressures this family is feeling? Maybe this is something to consider for your congregation.

Conclusions

Little research can be found to document problems of abuse and neglect related to the illness of the mother. It is, no doubt, a very small percentage of child abuse cases where this is a predominant factor. Add this, however, to lack of support systems, a rocky marital situation, and a tendency to lose control, and it becomes serious.

In our situation, the mother was not physically incapacitated, but her lack of energy and her active children affected her ability to function effectively as a mother and a wife. Some illnesses more than others place an overload on the emotions. When there are small children in the household, the stresses are increased.

Fortunately, in some situations, the mother can get help through support groups of other adults who are living with the same illness. If she is open to counseling, that might also help her deal with the family situation. Certainly an opportunity to be free from her children for short periods of time could help in relieving stress.

Other chronic illness, such as arthritis, have periods of pain which come and go, but the disease remains to add periodic stress to the household. The whole area of food allergies is just coming to be recognized. Some sufferers of severe food allergies say they have periods in which they feel as though they are "going crazy." Certainly that will add stress to a family.

It is worth noting that an acute illness of the mother or other caregiver may also precipitate abuse or neglect of the children. The shortness of the illness, however, makes it less likely to leave a lasting impression on the parent-child relationship. In both acute and chronic illness, the support and caring of friends is a significant force in relieving stress.

Mental Illness

Mental illness in itself is not a high risk factor for child abuse. Usually parents who are diagnosed as schizophrenic or manic depressive are under medication which keeps them relatively stable. In some cases, however, occasional hospitalization can cause disruption for the family. If there is an extended family that is supportive, hospitalization will be less disruptive than for a nuclear family lacking other caregivers.

In general, the children of such parents are at risk primarily when additional factors such as isolation, marital stress, financial problems, etc., are present, factors which may exacerbate the stress that these parents are under. It is very rare that one of these children is seriously abused.

Occasionally a person who suffers from one or another mental disease does not take the prescribed medication with regularity. When that happens, the person may hear voices or experience a manic episode. The children of such parents may then be at risk if the manic parent dreams up fantasies which the child is expected to act upon, or the parent hears voices which order a harmful act to be performed. There is nothing the lay person can do to prevent such occurrences other than to be sensitive to friends or neighbors who are known to suffer these diseases, and alert concerned relatives when stress becomes observable in the family.

Women in particular seem to be subject to depression, which may or may not be diagnosed and treated with medication by a psychiatrist. Whether the depression is generalized with no direct apparent cause, or situational in that it seems to be occurring due to particular circumstances the mother faces, the results are similar.

Children of such women may be victims of neglect. Neglect may take many forms, such as lack of proper nutrition and cleanliness, or lack of affection and warmth from the mother.

Women who suffer depression are, in general, an overlooked group. The family physician may provide placebos to keep them satisfied, or tell them that there is nothing wrong with them. Their pastor may tell them to have more faith and/or put more energy into being a "good" wife and mother.

When such mothers become severely depressed, they may sit around in their robes all day. They may have frequent headaches and stomach aches that keep them from performing the little tasks that keep a household going and children well cared for. These children may not receive nutritionally balanced meals, because mother is unable to pull herself together long enough to plan and prepare a full meal. They may fail to wear the proper clothing, because mother is not watching carefully as they go out to play. Perhaps the most common result of a mother's depression is her inability to provide the love and affection that children need.

Role Play

Choose someone to play the part of a depressed mother of two preschool children. Let her be resistant to suggestions for alleviating her situation.

Choose someone to play the part of a neighbor. Let the neighbor try to get this mother to do something rather than sit around all day and yell at the children.

Discussion: How did this work? What might work better? Rather than trying to tell this woman what she should do, try to be a listener. Let her tell you whatever she feels inclined to say. Ask her what she thinks would help.

What community resources are available to assist this mother? If she knows of someplace she could go for help, could you offer to go with her so as to soften the first encounter with something new?

Remember, you help the children by helping the mother feel good about herself. Could your church provide classes to help train potential listeners? What else might your church people think of doing that could assist the depressed and mentally ill parent?

Conclusions

Mental illness of the mother or major caregiver may be a significant factor in neglect of children. Neglect is an inability to provide for the physical and emotional needs of children. A woman's energies may be so wrapped up in depression that she has nothing to give her children. She may also be blind to the fact that her "illness" is affecting the children.

A mentally healthy spouse can help level out the family balance, although there would still be a strain. In most cases, it is best if families can remain together, but supports are needed to shore up what family strengths there are.

Information on abuse of children in these cases is not documented. However, if we are concerned about the self-esteem and growth of these children, we must be alert to potential neglect as well as abuse.

Substance Abuse

Alcohol is clearly implicated as a primary factor in abuse of spouse and children. In addition to the direct effects of the drinker who becomes abusive in language and behavior when under the influence, there are also indirect effects, such as the father who drinks and is abusive to mother, who is then abusive toward the children. There is also the parent who drinks and misses work frequently enough to affect the family income, and the parent who drinks and disappears.

Mother may be the drinker in the family. She may be abusive or totally passive when she drinks. In addition, when mother drinks heavily while she is pregnant, the baby may be born retarded or excessively small, subject to all the problems of early born infants.

The mother who compulsively drinks while also nursing her baby is probably indirectly subjecting the baby to the effects of alcohol. While there is still disagreement among pediatricians, organizations that work with women alcoholics assert that the drinking and nursing mother is harming her infant, and the small liver may be seriously injured by the alcohol that mother consumes.

The mother who frequently drinks herself into oblivion, is unable to change diapers, feed infants, watch toddlers, or any of the myriad other things that parents of small children must do. A supportive spouse can cover for some things, but if that spouse is away when these events occur, the child is a victim of severe neglect.

The effect of having a parent who uses various other drugs is unclear. We do know that use of drugs during pregnancy can cause a newborn to experience withdrawal symptoms at birth which can seriously affect the baby's health and well-being. Similarly, parents who use other dangerous drugs may be "unavailable" to provide for a child's needs in the same sense that an inebriated parent is unable to provide for those needs.

What organizations are available in your community to help such parents? Talk with a representative of your local Alcoholics Anonymous (AA) group. Find out what resources it has to help such a parent. Visit with a Children's Worker in your county to find out what legal recourse there might be to deal with alcoholic parents.

Remember that drug abuse and alcoholism rarely occur without a cause. While you or your group may feel inadequate to deal with these problems, you might be able to get a handle on family discord, depression, or other precursors of alcoholism and drug abuse. Brainstorm various influences that seem to lead people to become addicted to drugs or alcohol. Then brainstorm societal changes or resources that will need to be available as a preventive.

Conclusions

There has been some documentation to the effect that alcoholism is highly implicated in family violence. AA has a special program for children of alcoholics, and there are even books written to help family members deal with a parent's alcoholism. What is lacking is any study of the very young child's vulnerability to neglect or abuse by the alcoholic or substance abusive parent.

"The lack of research on the subject (women and alcoholism) is most striking."[1] Women are more likely to drink alone than are men. This is especially of concern when there are small children in the home. That issue is not addressed in the literature at all. "It would seem that for women, alcoholism is related to insecurity in the feminine role, dependency, low self-esteem, fear of inadequacy, and sensitization to loss."[2] This is a fairly accurate description of mothers who drink to excess, and may give us a handle on how to help them.

These families need our help. They are often isolated without friends or acquaintances. Often there is no belief system to sustain them in difficulty. Families who live like this may well be subjecting their children to continuing abuse and neglect. The consequences for them as well as for society can be tragic.

Summary

Parents, particularly mothers who suffer from mental illness, chronic physical illness, or alcoholism, are not always abusive to their children. More than likely, they will neglect their children. This needs to concern us as much as abusive behavior, although it is harder to deal with the issue. As concerned neighbors and friends, we need to be sensitive to extra stress in these families. When they have extended families who can help, we may need to alert them. If they do not, we need to have information about community resources readily accessible. In some cases, we may need to report the neglect to the child protection agency.

For Thought and Action

1. How would you react if someone you knew called frequently and kept you on the line nearly an hour relating his or her problems? What are some constructive ways you might handle the situation?

2. Do you have church members who seem to have a lot of problems? In what ways do you reach out to them?

3. Is there a system in your congregation whereby people volunteer to assist other members who are experiencing physical or emotional illness? Is there a cooperative arrangement that swings into place to care for small children when parents are ill? If not, how could such ministries be initiated?

4. Make a commitment to become better acquainted with some of your neighbors. Establish a network so that you can be alerted whenever they are feeling stress. Learn how to practice active listening[3] with them and provide emotional support when they need someone. Invite them to join you for worship and other church activities if they do not have a church of their own.

5. Ask a speaker to come from your local AA group. Inquire about the group's provisions for mothers of young children. What are their recommendations for drinking mothers of nursing infants?

Chapter Seven
Other Chronic Problems

Here in the final chapter of this section, we will look at two additional problems, families who experience repeated crises and parents who have personality problems.

Many of the situations that come to the attention of agencies seeking to prevent child abuse involve families who seem to experience crisis after crisis. Some families live lives akin to the most tragic soap opera. Actually, the family at-risk for abuse is more than likely also the family with multiple problems.

Some of the parents of these families are self-absorbed (narcissistic), having never resolved the issue of their adolescence when narcissism is a normal state. Some of them are angry at themselves and everyone else. Others expect their children to provide for their own need to be nurtured. Some are abnormally dependent, and some are pathological liars. Still others cannot hold down a job, or they tend to function outside the law. In short, these parents have personality problems, a category of disturbance that therapists are still not sure how to treat successfully.

Crisis-Prone Families

The crisis-prone family is not always poor. Even families on the upper end of the economic scale experience crises. While persons on the lower end are more likely to lack food and shelter, families on any economic level may experience marital, financial, and health crises.

There is little research available to explain what it is about some persons or families that seems to invite crisis after crisis. It is possible to speculate that they have come from families where crises have been part of the regular routine. The grown children in such cases expect that pattern to persist throughout their adult lives. Indeed, by their own unconscious acts, they create the very situations in which crises flourish. This fails to explain all cases, and unfortunately it does not help us understand how to help them break away from such patterning.

We do know that individuals subjected to frequent "double-bind" messages as children are less likely as adults to recognize the relationship between cause and effect. Recognition of the relationship between cause and effect is very important to making plans and carrying through so that good things can happen. When that relationship is not understood, plans are not made or not carried through, and crises are more likely to occur.

Communication Problems

"Double-bind" is communication in which the sender sets up a situation to which the receiver cannot react without being in the wrong according to the sender's instructions. Let us examine the aspects of communication in order to clarify "double-bind."

There are at least three aspects to communication: (1) content (information given), (2) meta-communication (that which is implied by tone of voice, body language, or has previously been understood in the relationship of the sender and the receiver), and (3) reception of the message (not necessarily clearly understood). There is usually an unspoken assumption that the receiver shares the same viewpoint as the sender. If this is not true, then the reception is likely to be faulty, preventing real communication from occurring.

Relationships develop over years of contact, and gradually "a set of rules has come into being which is outside the awareness of everybody concerned. These rules insure the stability of the system (family)."[1] The rules are concerned with who holds the power and the expectations based on past interaction.

Relationships

Relationship may be symmetrical (between equals) or complementary (between persons of unequal authority, experience, or wisdom). Examples of complementary relationships are parent/child, teacher/student, and doctor/patient. The *difference* between sender and receiver is emphasized. The persons with authority, experience, and wisdom define the relationship. Those lacking authority, experience, or wisdom accept the definition. Relationships between the same persons may at times be either complementary or symmetrical. Healthy relationships will be flexible.

Double-Bind

In symmetrical communications there is an unspoken inference that the receiver is the equal of the sender and deserving of respect. In complementary communication, the unspoken inference is that the sender is in possession of greater authority, experience, or wisdom than the receiver. If the receiving person accepts that inference, that person will usually accept what the sender says and attempt to comply.

Parents who assure a child, "You can tell us anything," and then proceed to blow up when the child tells them something they do not want to hear, make both parents and child victims of the "double-bind."

Some other obviously "double-bind" messages are, "You owe me respect," and, "Be spontaneous." What are the "double-binds" in these messages? Can you think of other "double-bind" messages? Share them with the group and discuss the traps they spring.

Other Miscommunications

There are other communication styles which may lead to confusing thought patterns in individuals who hear them often enough. "Disqualification"[2] is saying no without *really* saying it. For instance, one person may turn to another for confirmation, saying, "Isn't that so?" and the second person just does not answer, or evades the answer with an indirect reply, a generalization, or humor. That is disqualification.

The instance above is further complicated when one of the individuals is a child. "The ability to act upon understanding will be impaired when, for one reason or another, any indication of correct understanding comes under threat of punishment."[3] A child of abusive parents is vulnerable to punishment when communication is so muddy.

"Mind reading" is a process whereby one person completes the sentence of another. The assumption is that the second person knows the thoughts of the other and is authorized to speak for the first person. "Spokesmanship" is the process whereby one person answers for another and may even volunteer the services of the other person.[4]

Communication patterns may reflect the manner in which those who use them see life. If life is, indeed, a confusing experience where persons are "damned if they do and damned if they don't," and nothing seems to have a rhyme or reason, crises are inevitable. There must be a sense of cause and effect in order for a person to learn from experience.

One difficulty in trying to discover the reasons for crisis-oriented existence is that crisis-oriented families do not have a stable living situation. While they may contact a service agency for assistance during their crisis, they rarely stay in contact with the agency long enough for it to do the research necessary. Their mobility is an important reflection of their scattered lifestyle. Let us look at some situations illustrating multiple crises. Perhaps we will see how marital and financial crises can lead to child abuse and neglect.

Marital Crises

Crises of one kind or another are not uncommon in most marriages. When there are children, there is an even greater likelihood of marital stress from time to time. When, however, a marriage occurs between people who have life histories of crisis after crisis and who tend to give double-bind messages, the children may well be at risk for verbal and/or physical abuse.

Let us take a look at a situation in which the mother comes from a background where crises are frequent. Father comes from a stable family, but their messages to each other are filled with double-binds.

Role Play

The mother: Through no fault of her own, the mother in this situation has experienced many traumatic crises in her young life. Most of these crises had to do with loss of one kind or another.

The father: The father comes from a stable family where he was often cast in the role of helper. When they met, the father naturally wanted to help this woman who had suffered so many losses.

The children: There are two children born within the first two years of the marriage, now three and four years old. They are normal children— one boy, one girl—who are sometimes confused by the double-bind messages the parents send one another.

The situation: Father is working as an ambulance driver. He likes his job, as it provides opportunity to help people. Mother is a part-time worker at a fast food chain. She works because she prefers that to staying at home all day. The children are left at a day care center when both of the parents must work at the same time.

Mother often fears that father will leave her. He meets many women on his job. He often works overtime.

Father decides to take classes and become a paramedic. This means that, in addition to his work hours, he will be gone during class hours and must do homework in what spare time he has left. This upsets mother very much. She believes he is needed to work at home or to take her out occasionally. To deal with her fears and stress, mother nags a great deal. When that is not effective, she creates a problem to which he will have to give his attention.

This family faces a double-bind. Father gives the family the attention they need only when there is a crisis, and mother feels she must create a crisis to keep him from leaving her. When mother does this, the children as well as the parents suffer through a "battle royal." Father, who is normally a loving parent, becomes frustrated and angry.

This time the stresses at home have caused father to give up his plans to become a paramedic. This has been a dream of his for many years, and he is still finding it hard to give up that dream. The couple have a particularly bitter fight. Afterward mother loses her temper with one of the children. Using a ruler, she hits him several times, breaking the skin and causing injury that will require stitches.

Choose two people to play father and mother and another to be a worker whose job it is to find out what happened. Let the worker determine what the safest arrangement is for the children.

Discussion: What happened? Were the children removed from the family? What do you suppose would be the feelings of the children under such a solution? It is common for the children to believe that it is all their fault. Under what circumstances would they be allowed to return to their family? If they were left with the family, what safeguard is there that this situation will not repeat itself?

Since father gives a covert message that he will spend time with the family only when a crisis arises, and mother is fearful that he will leave her if she does not "need" him all the time, they are surely in a "no win" situation. The mother cannot "win" unless she is in crisis. The father cannot advance at work, and he certainly cannot "win" at home. Unfortunately, it is likely that these parents are also giving double-bind messages to their children.

What is your reaction to this particular situation? What is happening to the children? What would you like to see happen? How could it be possible for that to happen? What would you do if you were a friend or neighbor?

Financial Crises

There is an amazing number of families living on the edge of financial disaster. "Getting as much as one is entitled to through welfare, foodstamps, etc. . . . requires persistence, patience, tolerance, assertiveness, intelligence, resourcefulness, self-esteem and a willingness to overcome myriad road blocks. Most become discouraged, disheartened, frightened and angry."[5] There may, indeed, be some "welfare cheats"; there are likely many more who are entitled to welfare but are not receiving it. As a result, private social service agencies providing shelter and food for these people are overburdened.

The Frazee Community Center in San Bernardino, California, is typical of the non-governmental agencies that are trying to stay on top of the need. In 1980 it gave out an average of thirty boxes of food per month. The numbers rose dramatically in September 1982, when it gave 952 baskets. In November 1982, it gave 1797 baskets, and in December, 1262.[6] Other agencies run out of food and have to turn needy families away. People still come to the Sunbelt states and the Southwest expecting to find the land of opportunity. They soon discover that these areas too are suffering from a lack of employment opportunities and housing.

It is not unusual for whole families to move to totally unfamiliar areas with the hope of a better life. Even young families with tiny babies come, either running away from a difficult situation or searching for a better life.

If you heard about a family with a two-month-old baby that had come several thousand miles with the hope of work in your community only to find no work available, what would you suggest? Suppose they had no money, no friends, no relatives here? It happens!

What dangers do you imagine parents placed their baby in by fleeing across country in an old car that is now broken and beyond repair? According to Matthew, while still a babe, Jesus was taken by his parents to a foreign country. What dangers do you imagine they faced? How do you imagine they survived?

What agencies in your community can provide help for families down on their luck? Do you wonder if most of these people are "losers"? Does that mean that their children will grow up to follow the same pattern as their parents? If this is true it must be stopped, or we will have an increasing number of people who drift and never quite "make it."

Abused and Homeless

Now imagine a family with three toddlers, living in a motel room.

Father: This man is a Vietnam War veteran and an alcoholic who comes and goes at his own pleasure. He is often violent and beats up the mother.

Mother: The mother is from an Asian country and speaks little English. She is only twenty years old and feels utterly lost. She receives AFDC payments for her children, but that is not enough to pay for the motel room and buy food for a month. She knows no one in the area, so when she runs low on food she goes without and gives what she has to her children.

She is afraid to go to a shelter for battered women, because no one speaks her language. She is immobilized by her ambivalent fears that father will return to beat her again, or that he will never return. She fears an alien culture and fears that she is unequal to meet the needs of her children. She is even afraid to make a decision.

The children's needs: Make a list of kinds of stimulation and experiences preschool children need so as to encourage them to grow physically, socially, and intellectually. Is this mother able to provide such experiences under the circumstances? Would you call it neglect if the children were to continue to live under these conditions? Would you call it abuse for children to observe their father beating their mother?

Personality Problems

Parents are sometimes absorbed in themselves to the exclusion of their children. In these parents, unmet personality needs are preeminent. Often their expectations are that persons and circumstances around them need to change in order to make their lives better.

Many of them are angry at authorities and family members. They are alienated from their family of origin, impulsive, impatient, and have inappropriate expectations of their children.

Some parents seem to lack basic information regarding what they can reasonably expect of their children. A frequent comment heard while their children are still infants is, "At last I have something that belongs to me." Along with the sense of "owning" the babies is the expectation that the babies will appreciate the parents' affection and caring. When the infants express their own frustration by crying, the parents cannot tolerate them.

In some cases, parents look to toddlers to give them comfort when they are depressed. They think it is clever when their preschoolers hand them cigarettes and light them, or prepare a snack for them. When the children are older, they are expected to watch the young ones, and in general, perform duties beyond their years.

These children often are not given the opportunity to experience normal development from infancy through the childhood stages of autonomy and discovery of who they are. As a result, the individual enters adulthood ill prepared for intimacy, responsibility, dependability, and stability, all characteristics of mature adulthood. Many display personality problems which are difficult to change.

These grown-up children, now parents, may well be preoccupied in looking for someone to make up what they lacked in their growing years. Their "knight in shining armor" is expected to rescue them, or their "damsel in distress" is expected to look up to them and tell them how wonderful they are.

As adults, persons with personality problems may exhibit poor work habits, poor parenting skills, promiscuity, irritability, aggression, impulsivity, and even be involved in illegal activities.[7]

Role Play

A family is living out of their car. They are without money and food. There are two children, one two years old and the older four. They have come for help, and this is not the first time. Periodically they have been given shelter. The Child Abuse Protection Agency has had several reports on them but is unable to locate them, since they have no address.

The father: Father has no skills and is unable to find employment.

Lacking an address, the family is ineligible for welfare of any kind. Actually, the parents rather enjoy this type of existence.

The mother: In the past, mother has had a kidney removed, and is currently not very well. She moves slowly and deliberately. She is not a cook, so when she is offered food she only accepts what does not need to be prepared.

Action! Choose someone to play mother and someone to play father. Have them prepare by reading the descriptions above. Choose someone else to be a worker in an agency that has provided shelter and food for this family before. Have the worker probe their lifestyle to try to find out what keeps them from becoming established as a stable family.

If you are reading this on your own, brainstorm on paper. First "become" these parents and write down all the reasons they might have for the problems they face. Then brainstorm about possible solutions to their problems.

Discussion: What happened in your interview or brainstorm session? Investigate the feelings of the worker. Were any solutions reached? Chances are that the worker felt utterly frustrated. Perhaps the worker refused service, or perhaps the worker gave them shelter and food for the sake of the children. Discuss the situation in which the family received help and one in which they were turned away. You may feel that there is no adequate solution in this instance.

Parents such as these may never appear for regular counseling sessions. It is clear that the father will never be able to function as a stable breadwinner. Mother is unable to provide nutritious meals. They want no outside assistance toward changing their lifestyle. They refuse to cooperate with authorities who might be able to provide some services for the children. They would accept food, but if there are strings attached, they will ignore them.

It is easy to say that the parents have created their own dilemma, but we cannot dismiss the children so easily. Both parents have personality problems which keep them from becoming contributing members of society. These problems seriously affect the children. If mother chooses to live under these circumstances, so be it, but the children are dependent and unable to understand their own deprivation. While the children are not physically abused, they are missing both good nutrition and healthy parenting models to prepare them for adulthood.

Summary

As a culture, we are inured to tales of men and women who are losers, who drift from place to place and never seem to find their niche. More and more, we are finding that there are entire families who seem to be losers, who drift and can never seem to settle down long enough to provide a stable environment for the children.

It may be true that there are some people who do not want to be helped. Let us not forget, however, that when these persons are parents, they are setting patterns which their children may well duplicate when they become adults. We can only look forward to an increasing number of drifters and losers unless we, as a nation, take this seriously and find a way to assist them to break the pattern.

The crisis-prone family that is reasonably stable may be best served through trained volunteers who can learn skills in nurturing these "misfits" of society. Volunteers who are willing and able to invest the needed time and patience are an invaluable asset. Only if we believe that change is possible can we discover the key that will break the cycle of child abuse and neglect that these families perpetuate.

Many of the parents with personality problems may not be amenable to the usual style of counseling. In fact, professionally, we are only beginning to learn how to counsel them effectively. There is no doubt that programs for these individuals will cost money. We might even need to invest some risk money in developing new approaches before we learn what works. We must be willing to go through that trial period. The alternative of ignoring the problem will only make it worse. If we do not want further proliferation of this problem, we must start now to save the children who are our next generation of parents.

For Thought and Action

1. Conduct a brainstorming session in which everyone in the group calls out various ways of assisting families in crisis and those parents who exhibit personality problems. Without evaluating the logic or practical issues (such as financing), allow yourselves to "dream" about possibilities.

2. Still letting yourselves "dream" a little, select the one possibility mentioned during the brainstorm that you would most like to see happen. Find out how you, as a group of caring people, could make it happen. What would you need: money, volunteers, an old hotel, a

storage room, counselors? Where can you find these resources and how could you raise enough money?

3. Are there some other Christian groups in your town that could work with you on a project? Find out! Maybe they will come up with some of the money and volunteers if you can convince them of the need.

4. What shelters and food banks are available in your city? How do they determine who is eligible for their services? How can they help "losers" get back into the mainstream? Do they need volunteers, financial assistance? Ask someone from one of the programs to speak to your group about their services. Does it make more sense to help them increase their service or to start another project?

PART III
Our Response

The final section of this study book is designed to help you move from thought to action, from learning about child abuse to developing your own response.

Chapter Eight will acquaint you with various resources available in many communities to deal with the problems of child abuse and neglect. Use this guide as a springboard for learning about your own state, county, and community resources. Make an inventory of what is available. Discover where the gaps in services are and see what you can do to fill these.

Chapter Nine will help you consider how you, your group, and your congregation can become actively involved in preventing and responding to child abuse and neglect.

Chapter Eight
Resources for Intervention

As a nation, we have come a long way from that period when we looked the other way in cases of child abuse. The time when it was considered proper to beat our children has given way to the new period when we are beginning even to question the use of corporal punishment.

When child abuse first came to national attention in 1875 with the cases of Mary Ellen and other children, our national outrage against these parents was expressed through punitive measures.

In the past fifteen or more years, the attitude toward abusive parents has become a more supportive one of providing treatment, with the children returning to the home as soon as is practical.

There is little agreement on what approaches are most helpful with parents who are prone to abuse. Counseling, concrete services (homemaking, financial assistance, etc.), and education have all been used, but the results vary.

There are several different agencies in place to help the child. First, however, something or someone must bring the situation to the attention of an agency that can help.

Securing Help

The Hot Line

Most counties have a twenty-four hour Child Abuse Hot Line. These Hot Lines are staffed with professional social workers trained in crisis counseling and skilled at making determinations about the cases that are phoned in by professionals and concerned non-professionals.

Anyone may phone in reports or suspicions. Professionals such as counselors, physicians, nurses, teachers, child care workers, and clergy are required by law in a growing number of states to report any evidence or suspicion of physical abuse or neglect. If, at any time, it is discovered that one of these professionals knew about a case that they did not report, they become liable for arrest. This does not happen often, but it has happened.

It is often difficult and awkward for professionals to report on their clients. These relationships have been legally considered privileged communication. Concern about the prevalence of child abuse, however, has led many states to enact legislation that exempts the issue of child abuse from the usual confidentiality protection. Educational programs have been instituted to inform professionals of their duty, and they have become more sensitive to the issue.

In addition to these mandated professionals, the general public is urged to report any suspicions. Such reporters are not required to give their names, but they will be kept on the line long enough to get as clear a picture as possible about what is happening.

From 1980 to 1982 the monthly reports from one county's Child Abuse Hot Line increased from around 400 to more than double that amount. The severity ranged from verbal abuse through broken bones to death. Deaths documented as resulting from child abuse ran between seven and nine a year.[1]

When a phone report to the Hot Line indicates that the child is in imminent danger, the local police department is notified and an officer, a trained juvenile officer if one is available, will arrive on the scene as soon as possible, and definitely within two hours.

If the report indicates that there is no imminent danger of further abuse, a social worker with Child Protective Service (CPS) will investigate the situation within seventy-two hours.

The approach of the worker will be to recognize that the household is under stress. While checking such things as overall household cleanliness and personal hygiene of the children, the worker will be sensitive to what pressures the parents are experiencing. Only if the child shows evidence of battering or sexual abuse, or if the house or the child shows evidence of gross neglect, will plans be made to remove the child from the home. The social worker does not have the authority to remove the child, although the worker may call the police to perform that duty, if necessary.

The social worker attempts to help the parents resolve any issues that may be causing the household stress. If there is need for food, shelter, or other concrete services, the worker assists the parents in satisfying these needs. The workers will assess the parents' support network and make recommendations to help. The attitude is generally supportive and understanding.

Follow-up calls are made until the family situation improves or it becomes imperative to remove the child or children.

One serious dilemma for the CPS worker is the necessity of making judgments about whether children will be safe if left in the home. When children must be taken from home, even where they have been beaten, they tend to believe that they are responsible for doing something wrong. Removal is a traumatic experience for both children and parents. The law is clear where bruises, broken bones, or burns are in evidence and were more than likely inflicted by the parent. The law is less clear about potential abuse. Occasionally the news media report an incident where the worker left the child in the home, and the child was later severely beaten or killed. In some cases the social worker has been arrested for negligence in failing to see that the child was removed.

Police Departments

If your community does not have a child abuse hot line, or if time is of the essence to save a child from further beating, you should phone your local police. If Juvenile Officers are available, they are trained to intervene in a sensitive manner. They do not wear uniforms and they travel in unmarked cars. They carry authority of the law to arrest parents or take a child into protective custody.

When sexual abuse is suspected, the Juvenile Officers often team up with a social worker and a nurse. Together they gently encourage the child to talk about what happened. To assist in the process for the very young, they have sexually explicit dolls so the child may point out exactly what took place. Children often lack the vocabulary to correctly explain what occurred, and the dolls help in that regard. Usually, when the parents are implicated, this talk is held someplace other than the home. The report may have been made by the school or a day care center. Having the team question the child in another setting relieves the child of the pressure of having the guilty party present.

In an *emergency situation,* if Juvenile Officers are not available, the next best persons to talk with are regular police officers. They are in uniform and travel in marked police cars. They may or may not know how to be sensitive to the feelings of the child and the parents, but they can arrest parents and/or take the child into protective custody when it may be necessary for the safety of the child.

We are hearing more these days about sexual abuse of children in day care centers. When put in perspective, actually only a very few centers have been implicated. Parents, however, are advised to pick their day care center carefully, and to listen to what the children report about activities there. It is a sad commentary that we cannot trust that our children will receive loving care in such a center, just as it is sad to think that parents could harm their own children. Unfortunately, we live in a world where simple trust is not enough.

Cultural Issues

One of the concerns that has arisen since the influx of refugees from Southeast Asia centers around the differing cultural norms surrounding child rearing. The Vietnamese have a practice called "coining." It is a process used with certain illnesses in which warm wax is placed on the child's back on either side of the spine. A coin is pressed into the wax, and a black-and-blue mark results. At first, parents were arrested when such bruises were discovered at school. Later, there was an effort to reach the Vietnamese community with educational material explaining our laws and advising them not to use that practice in this country.

Other cultural groups new to this country have the belief that to beat their children is to show love. When we are struggling with teenage problems in this country, it is difficult to convince persons that our ways are better. These Southeast Asians hold family life as of supreme value. Their teenagers are attempting to make a transition to a new culture. Their youths, just as those from other cultural backgrounds, find that they no longer feel a part of their parents' culture, and they do not yet feel accepted by their peers in their new environment. It is not surprising that they break away from their close family ties, just as adolescents from other cultures do. Some of these youths become members of gangs in an effort to find acceptance. To their parents, any deviation from the old ways is threatening, and many parents fight to preserve these old ways in a new country.

Residential Facilities

When a police officer picks up a child who has been physically injured, that child may be taken directly to a hospital to determine the extent of the injury. Depending on the seriousness of the injury, the child may be kept there to recuperate.

If the child is not seriously injured, the child will probably be taken to a county residential care facility for dependent children. These facilities are available night and day to receive children who have no safe place to stay.

Each county deals with the problem of dependent children in a slightly different manner. Most counties, however, have some type of facility to receive children who are in need of shelter and care. Many such facilities are strained beyond their capacity to house these children adequately.

The facilities employ attendants who are available at all hours for the children, and where possible, counselors who work with the families. In facilities where the children are kept longer than two or three days, there are usually teachers to provide schooling as well as a nurse to assist with health problems.

In no way can these be considered "homes." They are institutions. No matter how hard staff try to make their stay less traumatic for the children, these are locked facilities with a lot of upset children. Volunteers help humanize the services. They have the time to relate in a friendly way to the children, something the staff has little time to do. This is an important dimension for the children.

With the increase in child abuse and neglect, the question is whether to build larger facilities, and how large is large enough. Some may argue that it would be better to develop more foster homes, but there are never enough people willing or able to provide foster care.

A child may remain at some county facilities up to thirty days. By that time, the child should have either been returned to his or her own home, or placed in a foster or group home.

In other counties, the receiving facility may be used for a maximum of seventy-two hours. By then the children must have been returned to their homes or be placed in foster care. Each county is different. Find out how the system works in your county.

Group Homes

Many states have group homes, facilities licensed to house five or more children. They usually have live-in houseparents and trained counselors to assist the children. They are often under contract to the county to provide services. Some of these homes are geared to deal with children who have behavior problems or are suicidal. They may attend local schools, or classes may be provided at the facility, depending on its size and location and the types of behavior problems.

Often the children are housed in small groups, which, with their houseparents, constitute "families." These are children who cannot return to their parents for one reason or another. Only a small percentage of them have families interested enough in the children to be involved in family therapy over a long term. Individual counseling and group therapy are frequently included in the children's treatment, and they may stay for a year or more.

Foster Homes

Foster homes are usually licensed by the county, according to state regulations. There are two basic areas for awarding certification: the parents and the facility.

The parents must be found to be physically and emotionally healthy, and they must obtain a criminal record clearance.[2] "The foster parents shall take reasonable measures to provide for the physical and emotional needs of each child and to protect each child against injury."[3] The foster parents must be physically and mentally capable of providing both care and supervision.

The facility must meet basic health and safety regulations. The yard may have a pool only if it is safely fenced. In some counties, bunk beds are not allowed, but children may share a bedroom. Children of school age must be of the same sex in order to share a room. Smoke detectors are required[4] and a disaster plan must be developed, so that all the children know what to do in case of a fire, earthquake, etc.[5] Each foster home is subject to an annual inspection by the licensing agency.[6]

Most counties do not expect the foster parents to have special training, even though the children they serve are likely to have emotional problems. Some counties, however, have required foster parents to attend classes of some kind. Adult education on child development or support groups for foster parents, held monthly in the homes of the foster parents themselves, may fulfill this exectation.

Voluntary Agencies

Crisis Nurseries

Voluntary agencies are relatively new. Each one is individual in nature, and guidelines as to who may use them are determined place by place.

Crisis nurseries are good examples of voluntary agencies. These nurseries provide shelter for preschool children as young as newly born, when the parents are under such stress that they cannot interact with the children in a reasonable, nonviolent manner. It is voluntary, because only the parents of their own free will can leave the children. Most of these shelters will not provide housing for children under county custody.

It is very difficult for parents to admit that they are close to being abusive to their children. It is very difficult for them to believe that the authorities will not intervene and take the children. In short, it takes considerable stress before parents will avail themselves of the opportunity for relief for themselves and their children.

There is some suspicion among non-professionals that parents will take advantage of these services for their own purposes. But experience has proven that parents willing to place their child in the hands of strangers and submit to their requirements for counseling services are not doing so to take inappropriate advantage of the service.

Many of these parents have been referred by children's workers who have been called to a home where abuse was suspected but not overt. They have no legal reason to remove the child, but they honestly believe that a short separation and some counseling might help to alleviate the crisis and assist the family in remaining together.

These agencies emphasize short-term placement. Ideally it should not be longer than a few days, with a two-week maximum. Small children need to be with their parents if at all possible.

Children who have been recently abused are usually not accepted at such agencies. In fact, the child care worker is prepared to examine the child carefully so as to determine if abuse has occurred. When such evidence is found, a proper report is made to authorities. The parents will have signed a statement to the effect that they understand such a report will be made if necessary.

Charges for the service vary from nursery to nursery. Expectations for the parents vary also.

Volunteers are in great demand with many such agencies. They may be used to assist the child care workers and counselors, in fund raising, on speaker's bureaus, on the Board of Directors, and/or the Advisory Board.

Adolescent Shelters

Another type of voluntary agency is the shelter for adolescents. This type of facility tries to maintain a homelike atmosphere, rather than a large institutional setting where great numbers of youngsters reside. Often these homes are filled with runaways. One of our national problems is teenage runaways who turn to prostitution or drugs to support themselves.

These shelters make an attempt to reconcile adolescents with their families or help them to explore other options. Although no statistics are available to prove it, evidence indicates that a high percentage of these adolescents have left home to get away from abusive families. Probably one-third of the girls in these shelters were sexually abused at home. The director of an agency that accepts adolescent girls through county placement recently stated that 99 percent of its girls had been sexually abused at home.

Volunteer Organizations

There is at least one county that supports a half-time director for volunteers who are willing to work with families who have abused or are likely to abuse their children. The volunteers are, for the most part, women who are willing to take a six-week training course to work with these families. They learn how to teach specific skills, such as budgeting; they learn some "do's and don't's" (for example, never to lend money to the client). Though not counselors, they are trained to help their clients share feelings and to respect clients' rights to confidentiality. The volunteers are supervised by a responsible professional working for the county or for the private agency that currently serves the client.

These volunteers work with a family over a long period. They deal with multi-problem families whose difficulties cannot easily be solved. These are families without support systems or extended families. They are families with medical, emotional, financial, and other types of problems. Often family members have personalities that make it difficult to resolve their problems. The volunteer must be patient and caring. These parents are not the easiest people in the world to work with, for they seem to create their own problems.

The volunteers are expected to contact their families at least once a week. Often, in emergency situations, volunteers are called upon by the families, and the volunteers have to make a choice whether to sacrifice their own plans in order to be available for their clients. In short, volunteering takes real dedication!

As mentioned previously, it is so far not clear how best to help these potentially abusive families. One fact, however, seems to be emerging:

Great success is often achieved through "the services of a lay person (volunteer trained on the job and supervised by a professional) who was assigned to the client to serve as a friend, support, and social contact."[7]

"Clients receiving lay services were . . . frequently reported to have reduced propensity to abuse or neglect their children."[8] This may be true because the professional does not have the time required to nurture and care for these parents who come from abusive families, are isolated, have medical problems, financial problems, and personality problems. A professional relationship is strictly complementary rather than symmetrical, whereas the relationship with the volunteer will fluctuate between complementary and symmetrical. The volunteer has the time and interest to be the friend and ally so desperately needed.

Parents Anonymous

Parents Anonymous (PA) is a self-help group for parents who have been abusive to their children. The local group may or may not have the services of a professional sponsor. The parents themselves, however, run the group. The group meeting is a safe place for members to share feelings of guilt and embarrassment over the way they have treated their children.

PA provides continuing support for parents to improve their parenting skills and ameliorate the effects other life problems have on their relationship with their children. In child abuse cases parents may be required by a court judgment to attend PA for a given period of time. It is a highly respected organization, which is found nationwide.

There are other self-help and professionally sponsored groups to deal with specific problems, such as the incestuous family. Each organization should be checked out with professionals in the field to discover whether it is effective in what it is trying to accomplish. Some groups have been suspected of coddling the abuser in such a way that the abuser does not accept responsibility for what he or she has done; therefore, change is less likely to occur. In such cases, the child remains in jeopardy of repeated abuse.

Summary

In any plan for prevention of child abuse and neglect, it is necessary to be fully aware of available resources. Each state and each county differs in its arrangements to care for these matters. The private agencies differ even within a given area.

There may be problems peculiar to a given section of the country, such as mass unemployment or cultural differences regarding child rearing. All these things must be taken into consideration. But there is no excuse for not knowing what help is available and being prepared to call upon these agencies when needed.

For Thought and Action

1. If, following your study of Chapter Three, you did not call the nearest Child Abuse Hot Line, do it now. Request information about the agency, and/or invite a speaker to come to your group.

2. Ask group members to make a survey of public and private agencies dealing with child abuse and neglect within your area. Contact each one to discover what volunteer services are needed. A volunteer bureau may be of help in preparing this information, but it is wise to check with the agency itself to be sure the bureau's information is up to date.

3. Ask other group members to put together an information packet containing details about agencies needing volunteers and about the types of volunteers needed. See that every adult in your church receives the packet. If possible, present the information at a church gathering in which members are encouraged to become volunteers on some level.

4. Find out about self-help groups for parents in your area. Ask representatives to come and speak to your congregation.

5. Share with your pastor what you have learned about child abuse and responsible agencies. He or she may be legally bound to report incidents of child abuse.

6. Assign someone to inquire about what is involved in becoming a foster parent. If there are foster parents in your church family, ask them to share their experience. Find out if the foster parents in your area have support groups to encourage and help one another over difficult situations. Encourage such a group if one is not already in action.

7. If one of the groups you contact is in need of a space to meet, agree to approach your church's Board of Trustees on its behalf, and recommend the provision of space on a regular basis for little or no cost to the nonprofit group.

8. Are there any serious gaps in public and private services for abused children in your area? Do you have any voluntary agencies for

children who are in danger of being abused? If not, perhaps a nucleus of concerned church members might begin to research the possibility of starting such an agency. Remember to look for professionals who have skills to help and other lay people who may not attend your church but are concerned and want to help.

Chapter Nine
The Congregation as a Change Agent

This study began with a look at the recent history of child abuse and a glimpse of the current problem. Statistical reports have been cited which indicate that the problem is increasing, not decreasing. As people of a loving God, we need to be concerned!

It is a natural reaction to be repulsed by the news of children being physically harmed or killed by parents or step-parents. Our hearts go out to the child and we cry out in rage against anyone who could be so heartless.

It is harder to get a feel for the numbers of children who are sexually abused, because this type of abuse is slower in coming to light. There are indications that sexual abuse is much more pervasive than ever dreamed likely. It is difficult for young children to tell on their parents or other relatives who sexually abuse them, because they lack the vocabulary to explain, and because they are dependent upon those same adults for shelter, food, and what love they provide. Unlike children who are physically abused and believe they deserve the treatment they receive, sexually abused youngsters often know deep down that this is not the normal way for adults and children to relate.

In some cases, there is no one who will believe them. As often as not, the family is well respected in the community, and the guilty father, brother, or uncle is law-abiding in every other respect. It may be that only after the child has grown to adulthood and is having difficulty in some other areas, the background of systematic sexual abuse will be revealed.

How many more children are verbally and psychologically abused, we can only guess. Many parents, some time or another, will be verbally abusive. We all fail as parents once in a while, but it is not the once-in-a-whiles that are of ultimate importance.

There are two points at which we must judge the need for prevention. First, a habitual style of verbal or psychological abuse destroys children's self-esteem and places them in constant double-binds, making their adjustment to responsible adulthood difficult, if not impossible.

This leads us to the second point: Not only are such children hurt physically, psychologically, sexually, but their future adulthood is dangerously hampered. There is little likelihood that these individuals can later have mutually satisfactory relationships with friends and their own children. Without the early models of parents who loved and cared about their children and provided opportunities for them to develop self-esteem, these new parents will likely repeat the same or similar parenting mistakes learned from their parents. This is a frightening fact, one that should not be overlooked. It can have serious implications for our whole nation.

What Can Be Done?

Our country has an unwritten philosophy that every child has the right to a loving home where childhood can be enjoyed and preparation for responsible adulthood learned. How do you suppose a policy reflecting this philosophy could be implemented? At what point should a child be removed from the family in order to attain such a goal? How long is "long enough" to wait for parents to improve their parenting skills? How can we teach parenting most effectively, and when? Is parenting best taught in a semester at school, or over many years and in many different ways, or both? Decisions about such matters are crucial to the forming of a policy which can lead to a generation of more skillful parents who are better able to demonstrate their love.

As Christians we must help make these decisions. We can keep our governmental representatives informed of our concerns and advise them of facts they may not have at hand. We can form advocacy groups and encourage implementation of programs to work on the problem.

In some towns and cities there is clearly a need for additional agencies to provide counseling to abusive families and shelter for abused children. In planning for future generations, we must not overlook the children of today. Prevention must be on two levels, planning for the future and dealing with today's problem.

More volunteers are needed. Professionals may offer their expertise, but it is the non-professional volunteer working directly with the children and the families who can make the ultimate difference. When a family suffers from multiple problems, relationships may not have a high priority and motivation to improve them may be low. This does not change the child's need to be a child and to have a loving and skillful parent. Volunteers who work with families can enter and be a part of such a family in a way no professional can.

When one or two people, or a thousand, understand the problem and the underlying factors, each can act as a friendly neighbor to help ease the load of the family next door who tends to berate their child, or report the abusive family to the authorities. This is not just someone else's problem; it is ours!

This book can help you discover what you and your congregation can do. Your awareness level has been raised by your study and discussion. Your ideas on how to create changes have developed through your group participation, brainstorming, and planning. This chapter will help you put it all together and come out with something that you, your group, your congregation, or your district can do to make a difference, a tangible demonstration that you care.

Church Projects

Advocacy

Your congregation needs to become informed and participate in some action. Those who are interested in policy decisions as a means of prevention, can be responsible for discovering what advocacy groups are already at work on the problem. Your church could send a representative to attend meetings and further stimulate such groups to think in new directions. These representatives could also secure literature regarding public policy and inform the congregation when legislation is coming up that needs the support of everyone.

If no advocacy group can be found, you can start one. Enlist the aid of professionals in the fields of child care, education, law, social work, and medicine; and become advocates for children on a national, state, and local scale.

Agency Sponsor

1. Child Abuse Council

Another posible project for your congregation is to initiate a Child Abuse Council, if none exists in your area. The council brings together all the agencies working in the field in an effort to share information and support. The council can be responsible for encouraging an informed population. It can sponsor workshops and speak through the local media. It can sponsor the training of volunteers, and can function as an additional advocacy group.

A Child Abuse Council may consist of representatives from Child Protective Services, the Child Abuse Hot Line, pediatricians, public health nursing, school nurses, social workers, agencies that work with abusive families, law enforcement, legal representatives, and churches. Monthly meetings allow opportunity to share information and act as a lobby group locally as well as statewide. A committee can keep track of the state laws that are changing and provide input into the system. An annual county-wide workshop sponsored by the council is a valid vehicle for informing teachers and other professionals of their responsibility for reporting and tell them about local resources to help families.

One Child Abuse Council sponsored a voluntary shelter for children with parents under stress and counseling for the parents. The professionals on this council wanted to help prevent abuse rather than just pick up the pieces afterward.

Such councils may or may not have the support of county administration. There are advantages to both positions. As a recognized function within the structure, cooperation of various public employees is assured. As an outside group, it is easier to be critical of county services, and lobby for change, if that is necessary.

2. Shelters

Shelters are usually small facilities designed to care for childlren or adolescents who are in need of a safe space for voluntary placement away from their families, other than the involuntary county homes or foster placement. Private, nonprofit groups sponsor the agencies and get them started. A dream, a practical planner, legal advice, and money to rent facilities and hire a professional staff are all needed to bring the shelter into existence. Many volunteer hours go into creating such a sanctuary.

Once the shelter is begun, volunteers are needed to supplement the staff and act as fund raisers. It is an ongoing nonprofit agency which needs dedicated persons to do the work. The hired staff can maintain the professional aspect of the agency, but volunteers are needed on the board, to assist the workers, and to serve as fund raisers.

A shelter is an expensive venture, but there are public and private grants available. Knowledge of such grants, funding sources, and the ability to write proposals is an essential aspect of the maintenance of services. The United Way may be a potential source of income after the agency has been established and operating for a number of years.

To start a shelter is not easy, but do not be overwhelmed. Just as in your garden you do a little at a time, so each member of a task force spades his or her section of the "garden" until it all gets done. Others will provide the fertilizer, and still others can water and remove the weeds. If there is no such shelter available and one is needed, who will do it if you do not? If no one does, what then?

3. Training Volunteers

At several places in this study, the use of volunteers who work with specific families has been mentioned. Statistics cited in Chapter Eight indicate that the most effective work being done with abusive families is being done by trained volunteers under professional supervision.

Does your area have an agency designed to train such volunteers? Are the Child Protective Service workers in your city or county using the persons who volunteer to help? If not, then perhaps your church group can meet with a CPS supervisor to see if CPS is open to this suggestion. Information about what and how to train might even be provided by the CPS.

What better place than the congregation is there to find people who care, people who are willing to give of themselves to families needing friends? Never set a small goal. If your church is small, look to other nearby churches to find the people who will make a commitment. Set criteria in terms of choosing the right people as volunteers. A religious faith as demonstrated in daily living is important, but a person who pushes his or her own religious or other values on others can be a destructive element in an already deteriorating situation. If such people want to volunteer, find them a place doing paper work or arranging the inservice training rather than introducing them to direct family service.

Set up a serious training schedule, and, with the help of professionals in CPS or nonprofit agencies, match the volunteers with the families. Whichever agency refers the client is expected to provide the supervision.

The Volunteer Training agency can provide periodic inservice training for the volunteers after their initial training has ended. An occasional lunch and yearly awards for outstanding volunteers provide the type of association and satisfaction that is needed for volunteers to maintain a long period in a difficult relationship. Volunteers are a precious resource, and as such, need to be treated with care. Their hours are logged and recognition given for service.

A congregation can provide space for the volunteer training agency. A church might also provide space for monthly socials for the parents and their volunteers. This encourages isolated parents to come out of isolation for a few hours. The children can stay in the nursery and the parents can be taught something to enhance their self-esteem. It may be a craft demonstration or workshop. The intent is to broaden the horizons of these parents and give them something interesting to think about. As a by-product, this benefits the children, too. When a parent is happy within, he or she is more likely to share that happiness with the children.

4. Parents' Day Out

Many congregations are already providing a Parents' Day Out service to their communities. To combat isolation in young parents, the church provides several hours of child care for a minimal cost, and/or shared child care responsibilities. The parents may be encouraged to take the day to get away on their own, or joint projects may be planned. In some cases, the program includes speakers who talk on parenting issues. This can be a true preventive program when it is open to any parent who wishes to take advantage of it, not just church members. Everyone needs a break, but parents are twenty-four-hour attendants unless they can afford sitters.

Individual Projects

Whether or not your congregation decides to work as a child advocate, or sponsor a council or shelter, you as an individual can determine to take a part in stopping the cycle of child abuse and neglect. You can assess your own abilities and interests and time, and make a decision to help on one level or another.

First, learn the system. Know what your local resources are. Use them. Report any evidence of child abuse or neglect that you observe. Be sensitive to particular stresses that affect your town, community, or neighborhood. Loss of job, divorce, illness, etc., can all be clues that a family is under stress. When you know what the local resources are that can provide food, shelter, and child care, you can share the information with your neighbors to whom it might be useful. Where appropriate, step in yourself to offer services temporarily. In both your church and community, use alert eyes and ears and a caring heart to add to your knowledge of resources, then respond to needs.

Volunteer

Avail yourself of opportunities to become a trained volunteer. If your interest and temperament are such that you want to work with the families directly, make the effort to contact a volunteer agency that can train you, assign you, and supervise you.

If you want to work with children, contact your county home for dependent children or voluntary agencies that shelter children. You can often arrange to work several hours per week at your convenience. These agencies, too, will provide the orientation necessary for you to do your job well. Remember that not every agency can provide you with the type of volunteer work you think you would like, so shop around. Some agencies seem to have an overabundance of volunteers, while others need them badly.

If you feel that you can provide a foster home and take in one or two children who have had to be removed from their families, find out what your state and local regulations require. If you have a family, talk it over with them. Can you comply with the necessary requirements? Do you have the emotional resources required to love and handle children who have been deeply hurt? New foster homes are always needed.

Do you have some professional expertise? Are you a lawyer, a teacher, a social worker, a physician, a nurse? Are you good at organization? Can you assist with paper work or secretarial services? All these skills are needed.

Help Yourself

If you are a parent, you can make an effort to improve your own parenting skills. You are not alone. Rarely is a family so successful in relationships that it cannot use more information and skills. There are trained people who know about parenting skills. They can come to your church and work with groups of parents on communicating clearly, improving discipline, and dealing with emotions of both parent and child.

There are movies and books available, but nothing takes the place of sharing and being given the opportunity to practice new skills. There are courses in Parent Effectiveness Training, Dreikurs' Logical Consequences, and many more. The important thing is to learn methods with which you can be comfortable and which are adaptable to your circumstances. No one technique will solve all your problems, but when you have more than one technique in your repertoire, you begin to develop options. You begin to see how you can communicate your love for children in a manner that they can comprehend, and which is mutually satisfying. You can begin to drop those actions which tend to alienate, even temporarily, other members of the family. When you learn to listen carefully to one another and give clear messages, alienation is less likely. You will find that the techniques work with adults as well as with children, and you will find that you like yourself better for using them.

There are other benefits from learning to listen and give clear messages. Your church family can use these skills. Committees and task forces that are hashing through difficult matters around which there is disagreement can learn how to communicate in such a way as to encourage unity rather than division.

Most of us think we know how to listen, but few of us do. We are so busy thinking about what we want to say, that we wait only long enough for a gap in the conversation so that we can jump in with our thoughts. Listening is a skill which can be acquired, but it does not come easily. In effect, when we learn to actively listen, we can enhance mental health in children, in other adults, and in ourselves.

Summary

Child abuse and neglect is a serious national problem. It will not improve or go away unless more of us are willing to do something about it. We must attack the problem on two levels: stop the abuse that is presently occurring, and prevent future abuse.

If this study has helped you think about the problem and has stirred you to action, it has done what was intended. This is a clear opportunity to go forth as God's agents right where you live. It is not necessary to travel to a foreign country or the other side of town. Child abuse affects all races, all economic levels, all neighborhoods. Each one of us is called to open our eyes, grow as an individual in our own relationships, and be an instrument of God's love where we live.

We can stop the cycle of child abuse!

For Thought and Action

1. Decide how you will present what you have learned to your congregation, and do it.

2. Form a task force to decide how your congregation can best implement some effort to prevent or respond to child abuse.

3. Investigate the various parenting courses available in your community. Decide on one and work it into your church schedule within the next six months. Make arrangements for additional courses as needed for parents.

4. Develop a plan whereby your church people can learn to listen better and give clearer messages to each other and their families.

5. In your group, have each person share how she or he can personally implement new learnings and convictions gained as a result of this study.

6. Do not just read this book and say you can do nothing. God calls you to act!

Glossary

Acute: Severe, but of short duration; not chronic; said of some diseases.

AFDC: Aid to Families with Dependent Children; government grant to needy families.

Agoraphobia: Literally means fear of the marketplace, now more often taken to mean a morbid fear of being among people in a public place.

At-risk: Infants or toddlers are described as being at-risk if a developmental lag is observed or if developmental, social, or emotional problems can be anticipated because of the failure of the mothering person and the child to enter into a growth-producing relationship. Families are at-risk if they exhibit factors which might lead to child abuse.

Bonding: A uniting force; tie; link. Currently used by mental health professionals to describe that relationship which is or is not cemented at birth between (especially) mother and infant, but also between father and infant.

CPS: Child Protective Service. The title of this unit of social workers varies from county to county. Its task is to protect children from abuse and neglect.

Chronic: Lasting a long time or recurring often; said of a disease and distinguished from *acute*. Continuing indefinitely; perpetual; constant.

Denial: Meaning a refusal to believe or accept evidence about oneself or family.

Double-bind: A communication in which the sender sets up a situation to which the receiver cannot react without being in the wrong according to the sender's instructions. (See Chapter Seven.)

Empirical: Relying or based on practical experience.

Exacerbate: To make more intense or sharp; aggravate.

Extended family: The nuclear family is father, mother, and children, all of whom live together. The extended family consists of these plus other relatives, who may live elsewhere but continue to play a significant part in the life of the nuclear family.

Failure to thrive: A diagnosis placed on an infant or small child who has not gained weight within a certain accepted range and whose head circumference has not increased within range. The diagnosis is confirmed when a child is kept at the hospital, given proper food and love, and proceeds to grow at an accelerated rate.

Meta-message: That communication which is implied by tone of voice, body language, or has previously been understood in the relationship of the sender and the receiver.

Primary prevention: Usually the education of persons to preclude the occurrences of a disease or problem. May include the giving of inoculations to protect against a disease. The clue is in the word *primary,* meaning before the problem or disease has become evident.

Projection: The unconscious act or process of ascribing to others one's own ideas, impulses, or emotions, especially when they are considered undesirable or cause anxiety.

Symbiosis: A relationship of mutual interdependence between persons or groups. Used in this context to refer to parent-child relationships that are so close that neither parents nor children are able to see themselves as individuals in their own right. Role reversal is common in symbiosis: the parents act like children and the children assume responsibilities beyond their years.

Resources

The following books are recommended for those interested in learning more about child abuse and neglect. Items cited "DR" are available from Discipleship Resources, 1908 Grand Avenue, P. O. Box 189, Nashville, Tennessee 37202. Others may be ordered through Cokesbury or other bookstores.

About Child Abuse (C. Bete, 1983). This booklet helps readers recognize the symptoms and understand the causes of child abuse. Also available in Spanish, under the title, *Sobre el Maltrato de los Niños*. (Both DR)

A Child Is Being Beaten, Naomi Feigelson Chase (New York: McGraw-Hill, 1975). A brief history of the problem, with a broad perspective. Case histories whet the reader's interest. Author shows that the indignities of our welfare system and poor housing are among the factors contributing to child abuse, and that society as a whole needs to deal with the problem.

An Approach to Preventing Child Abuse, Anne H. Cohn. (Order from National Committee for Prevention of Child Abuse, 332 Michigan Avenue, Suite 1250, Chicago, IL 60604.) Ideas for preventing and remediating child abuse and neglect.

It Shouldn't Hurt to Be a Child, Anne H. Cohn (National Committee for Prevention of Child Abuse, 332 S. Michigan Avenue, Suite 1250, Chicago, IL 60604). A leaflet for general education regarding the issues.

The Maltreated Child, Third Edition, Vincent J. Fontana and Douglas J. Besharow (Illinois: Charles C. Thomas, Publisher, 1977). A historical and diagnostic presentation, this book also deals with prevention, legal aspects, and includes case reports and pictures. It is for the serious student.

Sexual Abuse Prevention: A Study for Teenagers, Marie M. Fortune (United Church Press, 1984). A five-session course for junior and senior high youth. Helps them recognize and avoid abusive situations and deal with the effects of abuse among their peers. (DR)

Abuse in the Family: Breaking the Church's Silence, Peggy Halsey. (Contact Office of Ministries with Women in Crisis, National Division, United Methodist Board of Global Ministries, 475 Riverside Drive, Room 338, New York, NY 10115.) A mission/action study program of the United Methodist Board of Global Ministries.

The Battered Child, Ray E. Helfer and C. Henry Kempe, eds. (Chicago: The University of Chicago Press, 1974). Articles from various authors covering the history and demographics of child abuse. They deal with medical, psychological, and legal aspects. This book is for the serious student.

Sins of the Fathers, Ruth Inglis (New York: St. Martin's Press, 1978). The term *fathers* is used in the biblical sense, for it is the mothers as well as the fathers who abuse. Abuse is seen here as transmitted from generation to generation, and the author tends to blame it on the blindness and inadequacies of the parents. Chapters on therapy, divorce, and prevention.

The Abusing Family, Blair and Rita Justice (New York: Human Sciences Press, 1979). These authors use a transactional approach to treating abusive families, as well as Goal Attainment methods. The book is very readable. Half of it deals with treatment, and as such it is perhaps of greater interest to the professional.

The Broken Taboo, Blair and Rita Justice (New York: Human Sciences Press, 1979). One of the first books to examine the formerly hidden topic of incest. Authors tend to place more blame on the mother than is currently thought to be appropriate. Yet as an adult in the household, the mother must bear some responsibility for not knowing that incest is occurring and for not preventing it.

Coping with Abuse in the Family, Wesley R. Monfalcone (Philadelphia: The Westminster Press, 1980). A "Christian Care Book" for use by individuals or support groups. Helpful to both abused and abusers.

Cry Out! Inside the Terrifying World of an Abused Child, P. E. Quinn (Nashville: Abingdon Press, 1983). Reading like a novel, but true in its entirety, the story of this Christian counselor's childhood helps us become more sensitive to the experience of abuse.

The Best Kept Secret, Florence Rush (New Jersey: Prentice-Hall, Inc., 1980). This is an excellent and unforgettable book. It traces the history of sexual abuse from the early Hebrews and Greeks up through the Middle Ages and into today.

Books recommended to assist parents in raising well-adjusted children, at the same time keeping their own sanity and self-esteem intact:

Your Child's Self-Esteem, Dorothy Corkille Briggs (Garden City, NY: Doubleday, 1975). Helps parents create a strong feeling of self-worth in the child and to feel good about themselves. Recommended book for all parents of young children.

A New Approach to Discipline: Logical Consequences, Rudolf Dreikurs and Loren Grey (New York: Hawthorn Books, Inc., 1968). Rather than using traditional methods of child discipline, parents can be democratic. Part of this method is the use of logical consequence in disciplining children. Many examples.

Parent Effectiveness Training, Thomas Gordon (New York: New American Library, 1975). This book teaches successful methods of parent-child communication, methods that are clear and help both parent and child to feel good about themselves. It also includes a method of dealing with parent-child conflict in which neither parent nor child is a loser.

Notes

Chapter One

[1] Commission on the Status of Women, "Analysis: Women and the 1983/84 State Budget," *California Women* (March-April 1983): 3.
[2] Ibid., p. 5.
[3] Tribune Wire Service, "Democrats Offer 29 Bills Against Child Abuse," *The Tribune*, San Diego, 8 February 1984, p. A-8.
[4] Virginia R. Mollenkott, "Evangelicalism, Patriarchy, and the Abuse of Children," *Radix Magazine* (Jan.-Feb. 1982): 15.
[5] Ibid., p. 16.
[6] Ruth Inglis, *Sins of the Fathers* (New York: St. Martin's Press, 1978), p. 18.
[7] Ibid.
[8] Ray E. Helfer and C. Henry Kempe, Eds. *The Battered Child* (Chicago: The University of Chicago Press, 1974), p. 3.
[9] Ibid., p. 19.
[10] Mollenkott, "Evangelicalism," p. 15. (Cited from Dr. Robert ten Bensel, speaking at a conference on child abuse sponsored by the University of Minnesota, Minneapolis, 11 June 1981.)
[11] Ibid. (Cited from Dr. Elizabeth Kubler-Ross at a seminar by Omega Institute, Foxhollow, Lenox, MA, 6-7 June 1981.)
[12] Alvin Toffler, *Future Shock* (New York: Random House, 1970).
[13] Ariel Swartley, "If This Were Any Other Job, I'd Shove It," *Mother Jones*, 8 (May 1983): 36.
[14] Inglis, *Sins of the Fathers*, p. 34.
[15] Ibid., p. 35.
[16] Ibid., p. 36.
[17] Benjamin Spock, *The Common Sense Book of Baby and Child Care* (New York: Meredith Press, 1946).
[18] Neil Gilbert, "Policy Issues in Primary Prevention," *Social Work Journal*, 27 (July 1982): 294.
[19] Joseph A. Walsh, "Prevention in Mental Health Organization and Ideological Perspectives," *Social Work Journal* 27 (July 1982): 298.

Chapter Two

[1] Helfer and Kempe, *The Battered Child*, p. 43.
[2] Florence Rush, *The Best Kept Secret* (Englewood Cliffs, New Jersey: Prentice-Hall, Inc., 1980), p. 43.
[3] Ibid., p. 1. (Quote from Phillip Noble, Introduction to William Kramer & Others, *The Normal & Abnormal Love of Children* [Kansas City: Sheed Andrews & McMeel, Inc., 1976], p. ix.)
[4] Ibid.

5 Ibid. (Quote from Alan Guttmacher Institute Research and Development Division of Planned Parenthood, *One Million Teenagers* [New York, 1976], p. 10.)
6 Ibid., p. 6.
7 Ibid., p. 10.
8 Ibid., p. 2.
9 Rudolf Dreikurs and Loren Grey, *A New Approach to Discipline: Logical Consequences* (New York: Hawthorn Books, Inc., 1968), pp. 62-82.
10 Thomas Gordon, *Parent Effectiveness Training* (New York: New American Library, 1975), pp. 194-215.

Chapter Three

1 Doug Brown, "Agencies Push Prevention of Child Abuse," *Los Angeles Times* (5 November 1982) Part V, p. 26.
2 Susan L. Smith, "Significant Research Findings in the Etiology of Child Abuse," *Social Casework*, 65 (June 1984): 344, a quote from Winifred Scott "Attachment and Child Abuse: A Study of Social History Indicators Among Mothers of Abused Children," *Dissertation Abstract International* 35, 12-B (1974), p. 6113.
3 Mary Jane Green and Betty Orman, "Nurturing the Unnurtured," *Social Casework* 62 (September 1981): 399.
4 Ibid.
5 Norma Kolko Phillips, "Interventions with Hi-Risk Infants and Toddlers," *Social Casework* 63 (December 1982): 588, a quote from D. W. Winnicott, *The Maturational Process and the Facilitating Environment* (New York: International Universities Press, 1965).
6 Green and Orman, "Nurturing," p. 399.
7 Ibid.
8 Ibid., p. 400, a quote from Charles H. King, "Family Therapy with the Deprived Family," *Social Casework* 48 (April 1967): 203.
9 Joan M. Jones and R. L. McNeely, "Mothers Who Neglect and Those Who Do Not," *Social Casework* 61 (November 1980): 566.
10 Ibid.
11 Josephine A. Fraden, "Adopting the Abused Child: Love is Not Enough," *Social Casework* 62 (June 1981): 362-3.
12 Ibid., p. 363.

Chapter Four

1 Smith, "Significant Research," p. 339.
2 David B. Guralnik, Ed., *Webster's New World Dictionary of The American Language*, 2nd College Edition (New York: Simon & Schuster, 1980), p. 27.
3 Rita and Blair Justice, *The Abusing Family* (New York: Human Sciences Press, 1976), p. 69. A quote from B. F. Steele (as quoted by C. Henry Kempe, "Paediatric implications of the battered baby syndrome," *Archives of Diseases in Childhood* 46, February 1971, pp. 28-37).

⁴Ibid., pp. 69-70.
⁵Ibid., p. 70. Including quote from T.F.A. Plaut, *Alcohol Problems: A report to the nation by the Cooperative Commission on the Study of Alcoholism* (New York: Oxford University Press, 1967), p. 122.

Chapter Five

¹Phillips, "Interventions," p. 586 in reference to Erik H. Erikson, *Identity and the Life Cycle* (New York: International Universities Press, 1967) and Selma Frailberg, "The Origins of Human Bonds," *Commentary* 44 (December 1967): 47-57.
²Smith, "Significant Research," p. 342.
³Ibid.
⁴Edward R. Ritvo, ed., *Autism* (New York: Spectrum Publication, Inc., 1976), p. 287.
⁵Francis Turner, *Differential Diagnosis and Treatment in Social Work, Second Edition* (New York: The Free Press, 1976), p. 435.
⁶Ibid., p. 357.
⁷Ibid., p. 364.
⁸Ibid., p. 434.

Chapter Six

¹Marguerite L. Babcock and Bernadette Connor, "Sexism and Treatment of the Female Alcoholic: A Review," *Social Work* 25 (May 1981): 236.
²Lois Lester, "The Special Needs of the Female Alcoholic," *Social Casework* 63 (October 1982): 453.
³Thomas Gordon, *Parent Effectiveness Training* (New York: New American Library, 1975), pp. 29-102.

Chapter Seven

¹Paul Watzlawick, *An Anthology of Human Communication* (Palo Alto, CA: Science and Behavior Books, Inc., 1964), p. 5.
²Ibid., p. 18.
³Ibid., p. 38.
⁴Ibid., p. 54.
⁵Charles H. King, "Family Therapy with the Deprived Family," *Social Casework* 48 (April 1967): 203 as quoted by Green and Orman, "Nurturing the Unnurtured," p. 400.
⁶Linda Irby, Frazee Community Center, 1140 West Mill Street, San Bernardino, CA 92410.
⁷American Psychiatric Association, *Diagnostic and Statistical Manual of Mental Disorders, III Edition*, American Psychiatric Association, Washington D.C., 1980, pp. 320-21.

Chapter Eight

[1] Child Abuse Registry (CAR) Reports from July 1980 through June of 1982. Available from the Child Abuse Registry, Orange County, California.
[2] Dept. of Social Services, *Regulations Relating to Foster Family Homes*, Sacramento, CA, 1980. Sec. 85089.
[3] Ibid., Sec. 85121.
[4] Ibid., Sec. 85175.
[5] Ibid., Sec. 85147.
[6] Ibid., Sec. 85115.
[7] Anne Harris Cohn, "Effective Treatment of Child Abuse and Neglect," *Social Work Journal* 24 (November 1979): 516.
[8] Ibid.